YOU CAN LIVE HAPPILY MARRIED FOR A LIFETIME

Modern Applications of Proven,
Timeless Wisdom to Create
a Lasting, Successful Relationship

Wendy Fierstein
Mediator for Couples

BALBOA.
PRESS
A DIVISION OF HAY HOUSE

This book is a work of non-fiction. Unless otherwise noted, the author and the publisher make no explicit guarantees as to the accuracy of the information contained in this book and in some cases, names of people and places have been altered to protect their privacy.

Balboa Press books may be ordered through booksellers or by contacting:

Balboa Press
A Division of Hay House
1663 Liberty Drive
Bloomington, IN 47403
www.balboapress.com
1 (877) 407-4847

The author of this book does not dispense medical advice or prescribe the use of any technique as a form of treatment for physical, emotional, or medical problems without the advice of a physician, either directly or indirectly. The intent of the author is only to offer information of a general nature to help you in your quest for emotional and spiritual well-being. In the event you use any of the information in this book for yourself, which is your constitutional right, the author and the publisher assume no responsibility for your actions.

Print information available on the last page.

ISBN: 978-1-5043-6465-2 (sc)
ISBN: 978-1-5043-6466-9 (hc)
ISBN: 978-1-5043-6467-6 (e)

Library of Congress Control Number: 2016913470

Balboa Press rev. date: 09/16/2016

Contents

My deepest appreciation to the following people
for their guidance and support:

Harry Cohen, MD

Sandra Riediger, RN, DC

Lynne Walker, PharmD, DHom, LAc

Eva Kurtz, MA

Rabbi Zushe Cunin

and, most important,

my husband, my life mate

I am so grateful
to the Source of all wisdom.

♥

This book is dedicated
to the children where there is conflict in the home.

About the Author

At a very young age, Wendy Fierstein became interested in observing the relationships of couples in her environment. Her natural tendency as a peacemaker enabled her to see, though she did not yet understand, the mercurial potential of marriage.

The shockingly high divorce rate saddened Wendy but also inspired her to utilize her peacemaking abilities.

Over the past thirty years, Wendy became a mediator through the Los Angeles County Bar Association; studied leadership, management, and communication skills at UCLA; and studied psychology and neurolinguistic programming. She has researched health and nutrition since 1985 and esoteric teachings since 1989. She is a certified medical qigong instructor.

Over the years, Wendy has studied the works of many experts in the field of marriage—reading numerous books and attending many courses, lectures, and seminars that have provided her with an abundance of knowledge. Ultimately she became a mediator to help couples revitalize their marriage.

In 2002, Wendy created the *Peace and Harmony Technique*™ to help couples overcome the challenges that prevent relationships from reaching their potential.

This book is the culmination of twenty-five years of research. Wendy and her husband have been married since 1982.

Introduction

With a resounding *yes*, I can excitedly say that you *can* be happily married for a lifetime—and yes, you *can* achieve peace and harmony in your relationship.

Marriage really does work!

During my many years of study, I came across our ancestors' teachings concerning relationships. This book is a collection of my interpretations of these teachings. It's like having *a manual or blueprint* that will show you how to navigate your marriage. What I truly love about these suggestions is that they are simple, gentle, and kind, but at the same time, they have the most profound, positive effect that you could ever imagine.

This book will be immensely helpful for couples at every stage of their marital journey. It will help them improve their marriage and resolve challenges that are preventing their relationship from being harmonious.

With marriage, as with anything else in life, we need to know how to proceed in order to succeed.

I have applied these teachings in my own marriage, and I have seen for myself that they can renew and revitalize a relationship. I have interviewed many couples and observed that these suggestions worked successfully for the majority of them.

Sadly, the divorce rate is astoundingly high, and only a small percentage of couples who remain married can say that they are truly happy. When it comes to consecutive marriages, the divorce rate appears to be even higher! What are we doing wrong?

Different ideas, methods, and suggestions have been put forth by our modern-day "relationship gurus," but not many of them seem to help people create a successful marriage.

Numerous books have been written about marriage, but how can we know which ones are helpful?

This is that one good book that will save you from having to read so many others just to learn a few good points. Even more important, this is the book that will help your marriage reach its full potential. After all, who knows us better than the One who created us?

The names of actual people in this book have been changed to protect their privacy. Readers are responsible for how these suggestions are applied in their own marriage.

You may notice that in this book I repeat certain ideas. That's simply because it is so very important that you understand and implement this information. I've tried to keep my writing clear and concise, without any superfluous words, so my suggestions can be clearly understood. I want with all my heart for your initial intentions regarding your marriage to be fulfilled.

I am confident that after reading this book, you will be empowered with the knowledge to create a loving, peaceful, and harmonious marital journey.

You can live happily married for a lifetime.

With love and gratitude,

Wendy

Chapter 1

In the Beginning

There they stand, under a canopy of vibrant flowers—the dashingly handsome groom and his glowing bride with her long, white gown. They gaze into each other's eyes, oblivious to everyone else in the room. Their guests are bathed in the aura of their overflowing love. Then, a beautiful, golden light that seems to descend from the heavens envelops them, surrounding them completely. Suddenly, a booming yet comforting voice emanates from the light, saying, "You are now united as one."

♥

What if you knew without a doubt, as does our romance-novel couple above, that when you get married, your soul bonds with that of your beloved?

Our ancestors knew it. When they became newlyweds, they learned that marriage was a Sacred Vow, a bonding of the souls. Guided by their wise elders, they built strong family units that were fundamental to their survival and, consequently, a peaceful society.

At some point in history, our ancestors stopped sharing this important knowledge with the generations that followed. Over time, these marital treasures were forgotten, and married couples no longer had the guidance they provided.

Fortunately for us, this timeless wisdom is being revealed once again through esoteric teachings from sources such as kabbalah and Edgar Cayce (known as America's Sleeping Prophet). This knowledge will help you find the obstacles preventing your relationship from reaching its full potential, and understand how to correct them.

We all want to know how to handle our marital challenges efficiently so that our relationship will be strengthened and not damaged. In this chapter, you will learn why misunderstandings happen. Chapters 2, 3, and 4 will prepare you for chapter 5, "The Mighty Challenge," which explains how to resolve and defuse any disagreements or discord that might arise. Chapters 6 and 7 will guide you in reigniting the passion in your relationship to make it last happily for a lifetime.

Unfortunately, many people today are choosing not to get married, proclaiming that marriage doesn't work. But with the guidance that our ancestors once had, marriage definitely works!

Most people get married because they have dreams of sharing their lives with the one they love, of growing old together. After a while, however, some couples feel so frustrated and disappointed that they say, "I just can't do it anymore. My marriage doesn't work." The foundation of their marriage has been damaged, and eventually the couple feels burned out. This is not an uncommon problem, and it doesn't mean their marriage is coming to an end. All it means is that they need to pay attention to their relationship.

The information that follows will help you and your spouse build your dream together. It will help you transform your marriage into one that will make you both feel safe and loved. It will enable you to navigate the ups and downs of life together.

You will also learn how to create a relationship based on a foundation of love, trust, respect, commitment, and harmony, making your marriage a "rock" in your life. This rock will be sustaining, supportive, and vital, and it will continue to get stronger so it lasts for a lifetime.

All relationships go through rough patches. When this happens, successful couples tend not to ignore or exacerbate the problem. Instead they immediately work on resolving it in order to bring their marriage back into alignment as soon as possible.

The Mystical Side of Marriage

*A key to successful marriage is realizing
that you were given the ability to find your
life mate—your amazing spouse.*

The person whom you choose, and who chooses you for love, is your life mate. Your partner will help you grow and achieve your full potential to become the person you were meant to be.

We all have unconscious tendencies that must be transformed if we wish to reach our full potential. When you change those personality traits, you will begin to love and respect yourself more than you ever could have imagined. In response to that, your marriage will dramatically improve and your love and respect for your spouse will flourish.

These negative personality patterns do not reflect your true self, but they can inhibit necessary growth. They are so powerful that they can hold you back and sabotage your potential.

*In a relationship, these patterns manifest
themselves in the form of a challenge—
arguments, discord, misunderstandings,
miscommunications, frustration, and so on.*

Your spouse has the ability to help you connect with the positive attributes of your true nature, such as gentleness, patience, understanding, kindness, acceptance, compassion, empathy, willingness, generosity, tolerance, self-awareness, unselfish love, growth, helpfulness, and peacefulness.

We are all well aware of the harshness that occurs in the world today. Marriage teaches us to value and respect the life of another. All esoteric teachings encourage us to express gentleness in this world.

*A key to successful marriage is realizing that your spouse
is the one who will help you reveal your true nature.*

We need a partner in a committed relationship with a Sacred Vow to help us become more self-aware. When we transform our negative patterns, we grow. The more we grow, the happier and more content with life we become.

United We Stand

A key to successful marriage is realizing that you are more powerful in this world when you are united with your life mate than when you are single.

When you are invested in your marriage, you are mentally and emotionally stronger and healthier. You are also happier, and happiness increases longevity and quality of life.

The truth is, love is a force that is always there between a couple, so no matter how distant partners become, there is always a way for them to reunite.

Relationships need attention and nurturing, just like gardens. Beautiful flowers need water, nourishment, and weeding. If we don't provide these things regularly and consistently, the weeds take over and the garden loses its vitality.

In the same way, we can't get married and let the rest take care of itself. The success or failure of a relationship depends on how much is put into it. We invest so much attention and energy in accumulating material things, creating successful careers, finding good schools for our kids, keeping our environment healthy, and so forth. If we made the same kind of effort in our marriages, they would thrive.

When you find love, it benefits *you* to consistently nurture and strengthen it, molding it into the "rock" in your life.

Marriage is a work in progress, and it is the most important work you will do in your life.

The amount and quality of effort you put into your marriage represent your investment in a loving and harmonious future. Know with certainty that you can create a relationship that brings you happiness and fulfills your expectations.

Chapter 2

Know Yourself

There she sits in the stillness of the room, her breath quickening as the thought of him enters her mind. Her love for him rises like a rippling wave cresting in a glistening ocean. She quietly wonders what more can she do for him, for them, for their marriage. After some musing, a smile spreads across her soft face. She knows exactly what to do. She hurries from the room to seek him out.

♥

All teachings inform us that we are on this earth for a purpose: to contribute to society in our own special and unique way so that this world will become more loving and peaceful. We must learn, grow, and help others. Each and every person is important and vital, because no one else can bring light into this world the way that he or she can.

A key to successful marriage is improving yourself. Then your relationship will automatically change for the better.

People react to the energy that you send out. This energy comes from your beliefs, thoughts, and attitudes. You can change the way people respond to you by becoming self-aware.

I've heard so many people say that if their spouse would just change his or her ways, their marriage would be perfect. But trying to control your partner to suit your needs will create discord. The only things you can change are yourself and your reactions. When you use your thoughts, speech, and actions in a

6

more positive and loving manner, your partner will likely respond in kind.

A relationship will not improve if the things causing its decline continue. Hoping that things will change will not work either. Don't expect or wait for your spouse to "wake up" and rectify his or her behavior; *you* must be the initiator.

These suggestions are not intended to imply that you need to change who you are to suit the needs of your spouse, or vice versa. Instead, what must be transformed are the habits and dispositions that interfere with the peace and harmony of your marriage and cause negative experiences in your own life. These negative tendencies are behind most of the challenges that develop in a marital relationship.

The Transformation

Many people have come to me saying that they are confused and don't know what to do about their marriage. They thought that they had chosen a partner with whom they had so much in common; now things seem to have changed, and they feel they have made a mistake. After I explain the mystical side of marriage, most people have a better understanding of their situation.

Most of us are comfortable remaining as we are. The status quo is familiar. But some of the patterns that we unconsciously follow are misleading. They create negative experiences for our loved ones and for us. It's important not to ignore this fact, because if you do, you can't connect with who you truly are.

To help guide you throughout your day, begin each morning with gratitude for all the good in your life. This opens you up to receive even more things to be grateful for.

In order to transform yourself, you must always be willing to grow—to expand mentally and emotionally. You will be amazed at the joy you will experience by overcoming your negative patterns and living from your true nature! I have experienced it myself, and I can tell you that it is a feeling of *immense* satisfaction.

As I previously mentioned, we are given the ability to know who will be the most suitable partner to help us overcome these imperfections. Your life mate may knowingly or *unknowingly* present your hidden patterns to you for reviewing—which may cause you some discomfort and resentfulness, making it easy to blame your partner for the distress that often comes with growth.

Each of us holds misperceptions created from our previous life experiences, and we live our lives by them. This encourages disharmony until we become self-aware. Esoteric teachings state that we must eventually face our negative tendencies. The safest environment in which to do this is a marriage with a Sacred Vow and with the help of our amazing life mate.

People who are not aware of this dynamic might give up on their marriage prematurely, saying that marriage was not what they expected ("It's too hard!"). Unbeknownst to them, what they are actually doing is attempting to disregard those parts of themselves that created the negativity. Even if they were to choose another partner or move to a different country or take a different job, their unconscious patterns would still be there and produce problems in their lives.

As you can now see, it really benefits *you* to be open and willing to hear "messages" from your spouse, and to continuously strive to become more enlightened.

Self-Knowledge

We know for a fact that no one is created perfect. Gaining self-enlightenment is always an easier path to take than hearing how imperfect you are from someone else.

Besides listening to important messages from your partner, another way to gain self-knowledge is by observing your "self"—trying to see yourself the way others see you. (We naturally perceive ourselves very differently from how others perceive us.) While communicating with others, observe your own body language, attitude, tone, thoughts, and words. At first that might be distracting, but with practice it will become second nature.

A friend of mine moved to a new community, joining its social club so she could get to know her new neighbors. For two months she had trouble integrating, and she told me that her neighbors were not as friendly as she had hoped they would be.

I suggested that she try observing her "self." At the next social event, she observed her own feelings, thoughts, and her actions while interacting with people. She focused internally instead of externally.

To her shock and surprise, she realized that she had been behaving in a way that made her seem unapproachable. She observed that she may have presented herself as being "aloof". As soon as she understood that the problem was within her, she changed her thoughts and actions. At the very next club meeting, she had absolutely no trouble integrating into her new community of friendly neighbors.

Verbal and Nonverbal Communication

We generally express ourselves in four different ways: through speech (words, tones, and sounds); through body language (postures, facial expressions, and head and hand gestures); through actions (which reflect our attitudes); and through writing.

Words

Words are very powerful. They have the power to create an everlasting love or a growing distance between spouses. They can heal, build, or destroy. We must be responsible with our words. Most likely there will be a better outcome if we think before we speak.

When you speak to your spouse, think about how your words will affect him or her and how you would feel if you were on the receiving end of the same words. It helps to monitor your speech and listen to your tone. Do you sound harsh, impatient, or angry, or do you sound kind and loving? Do you filter your speech, or do you just blurt out whatever is on your mind, not realizing that you may feel different tomorrow? Once your words are heard, you can't take them back. You wouldn't want to hurt your loved one's feelings. Discretion with words is imperative.

Body Language

Nonverbal communication can sometimes be more important than words. After a meltdown with your spouse, you may wonder, *What just happened?* The real problem could have been the nonverbal communication.

For example, you may unknowingly have a habit of placing your hands on your hips while speaking to your spouse—to some people, this posture is an indication of criticism or confrontation. Your partner could assume that there's an underlying message in your body language, that you are being critical or confrontational, even if you are not. This may cause him or her to react negatively to what you said.

Kind Attitude

A kind and positive attitude usually attracts people, while a contrary attitude pushes people away. Are you relating to your spouse with a contrary attitude, or are you warm and gentle?

> *Even if you don't feel loving at any given moment, you can still be kind. Your thoughts and attitudes are not as private as you think. Realize that everyone picks up on the unspoken feelings behind the words.*

Our attitudes are initiated by our thoughts. To help you realize how powerful your thoughts are, try this:

Close your eyes and think about all the things that you really love about your spouse. Think about when you first met, when you felt those excited little prickles all over and you couldn't take your eyes off your loved one. You couldn't concentrate on your work because your thoughts constantly returned to this intriguing person.

When you are done, and if you had the right intentions, you will probably feel like giving your spouse a hug filled with love. Go for it—don't hold back! Your life mate will love it, and love you even more.

Communicating successfully all depends on *how* it is done, from the initial thoughts to the tone of voice, attitude, and body language, as well as the actual words.

Communication Habits

Becoming aware of the communication habits you learned very early in your childhood, from your parents and everyone else in your environment, benefits you and your marriage. All of us learn good and bad habits that may have been passed down from generation to generation. We become so practiced in these habits that by the time we are adults, it seems normal to us to communicate that way.

Here are some communication habits that must be transformed:

- becoming frustrated instead of using appropriate words
- getting upset before understanding the whole situation
- being impatient
- criticizing and complaining instead of directly asking for change
- being disparaging or rolling your eyes instead of being understanding
- being sarcastic and hurtful rather than compassionate and kind
- being quick to judge instead of listening first
- being stubborn in your position instead of being open-minded
- being closed to your spouse's point of view

11

- avoiding problem solving
- believing that you are usually right
- interrupting
- having a combative tone
- thinking about what you are going to say next while your partner is talking

To prevent misunderstandings and miscommunication, you must work on eliminating habits that create disharmony and improving skills that facilitate peace in a marriage.

Thinking Habits

Besides nonverbal and verbal communication habits, we also have thinking habits.

Most of our perceptions and beliefs were developed when we were very young, and some may not serve us very well in our adult lives. Listen very carefully to your thoughts, because chances are you are so used to hearing them that you've became oblivious to them. Even though you may not be aware of their existence, they still direct your speech and actions.

Thinking something does not necessarily make it true.
Therefore, reviewing your thoughts before you speak
or act will in many instances prevent a disagreement.

Constantly check your thoughts to make sure that you are consciously choosing positive and constructive ideas. It has been said that most of the stress we experience in life is caused by our imagination (thoughts), not by reality.

A key to successful marriage is realizing that when
you're communicating with your spouse, your thoughts
are as important as your speech and actions.

Thoughts are where our speech, attitudes, and actions begin. The way you present yourself literally all starts in the mind.

If you have contrary perceptions and beliefs, you will develop mental habits that cause negative thinking. What you think affects the way you feel, and what you feel translates into your behavior. You can enhance your life by continuously listening to what you are telling yourself and then changing your negative thoughts to positive ones. Reframing your thinking changes everything.

If you feel that you are having a bad day, you can be sure that your thoughts have been negative. You can immediately change the way your day is going by feeling grateful for the good things—even the simplest ones—in your life.

To break a bad habit, you must replace it with a new good habit that you practice consistently and persistently until it feels natural. The negative mind habits will always be there, so it's necessary to be vigilant in making sure that your thoughts remain positive. The more you practice, the easier it will become. When you implement these new, positive ways in your everyday life, they will become more natural to you.

A key to successful marriage is realizing that your thoughts are reflected in your behavior. No matter what words you say, your spouse will read the message between the lines and react to that.

If you get into the habit of thinking negatively about your spouse, your actions toward him or her will be contrary. It's very difficult to be sweet on the outside if you feel sour on the inside.

A very easy way to instantly switch from negative to positive thinking is to remember all the things for which you are grateful in your life mate. Doing so immediately transforms the way you feel, and as a result, your thought process will change.

Try practicing new habits like these with your spouse:

- Show appreciation instead of complaining.
- Compliment instead of criticizing.
- Speak kindly instead of being coarse.

You can get extremely helpful information on why and how to change negative thinking habits by visiting *DrWayneDyer.com*.

If you reframe your thoughts to be more positive,
you will change your life for the better.

Negative Speech

Unfortunately, profanity and gossip seem to be a part of our contemporary language.

The dictionary describes profanity as "profane language." Profane means "disrespect or contempt for the sacred; desecrate; debase; defile." Debase means "lowering of character quality/ dignity; cheapen." Debasing yourself or the person with whom you are speaking is disempowering. It is a hostile form of communication and creates the opposite of peace and harmony. More important, it creates a negative marital cycle.

Together we can make the world a better place just by choosing not to gossip or use profane language, especially toward our life mates.

Know Your Needs

To know yourself, you must know what your needs are. If *you* do not know, your partner won't either. Expecting a loved one to be a mind reader may create disappointment. In order for your needs to be heard and met, you must express them, making sure that your spouse understands.

If you are not sure what your needs are, start making a list of things that you would like. Here are some examples:

- I need fifteen minutes to relax when I get home before dealing with anything.
- I need help cleaning up the kitchen.
- I need to be spoken to with respect and kindness.

- I need to hear please and thank you when asked for a favor so that I don't feel taken for granted.
- I need to live in a neat and clean house.
- I need honesty in my relationship.
- I need to feel I can trust my spouse.
- I need to feel safe in my relationship.
- I need gentleness and tenderness from my spouse.
- I need our home to be filled with peace and harmony.

Once you know what your needs are, you can share them with your life partner. You can also ask him or her to do the same. Once you know what your spouse's needs are, you can demonstrate your love by trying to fulfill those needs.

Moods

Being aware of your moods is a big help in keeping the peace. After all, we are human, and sometimes we may feel "off" for whatever reason. If you are feeling cranky, it's worth making a special effort not to take it out on your spouse. It is very unpleasant to be around a moody person; you don't know what to expect from one moment to the next. It's always to your advantage to transform a cranky mood as soon as possible.

Here are some good ways to change your mood:

- Take a walk.
- Read.
- Practice deep breathing.
- Make a cup of calming tea.
- Feel grateful.
- Call a friend and talk about something other than complaints about your spouse.

Anything that is helpful to snap out of a negative mood is also helpful to your relationship.

Remember the Golden Rule: "Do unto others as you would have them do unto you." It's not a good feeling when your spouse takes his or her bad mood out on you, so don't take your moodiness out on your spouse.

When your spouse is feeling sensitive, choose words and tones that will defuse and not escalate any negative situation, such as

- "Are you feeling okay today?" When asked with concern, this question can help defuse a bad mood.
- "Can I get you some calming tea to help you feel better?"
- "If there's something bothering you, we can talk about it if you want, but please don't take your frustrations out on me." If you express this in a calm manner, you may help resolve your partner's frustration.

Be aware of your tone; keep it neutral. A combative tone will escalate the situation, and any criticism at this point may create a full-blown argument. Sometimes it helps simply to give your spouse space and time to relax.

Shanon

Shanon told me that she couldn't understand why she and her husband got into "huge battles" every now and then; they just seemed to happen out of the blue. With some investigation, we discovered that whenever Shanon visited or communicated with her family members, she would become irritable. From one to three days later, she and her husband would have one of their "huge battles." Shanon's family seemed to cause her to have extreme anxiety that would manifest in an argument with her husband.

I suggested that Shanon become aware of her emotions so that she could avoid any damaging arguments with her husband. I also pointed out that it would be beneficial to explain the situation to her husband so he could help calm her anxiety.

Their Point of View

Another way we can improve ourselves is by always trying to see our spouse's point of view. By trying to understand his or her thinking, we can resolve or even avoid challenges. Our partner's point of view is valid, and we must not disregard it just because we don't agree with it.

Resist the temptation to jump to conclusions and judge prematurely. If you know only your side of the story, then you don't know the whole story. Before judging, wait to hear your partner's side.

You can also remind your spouse to try and see your point of view by starting your sentence with "I hope that you will try and see my point of view. This is how I feel."

Self-Esteem

Self-esteem is very important to a relationship. You must have the courage to ask your spouse, in a way that will preserve your marriage, to stop doing things that you consider harmful to your relationship.

You must not be afraid of your spouse's reaction. If you express yourself in a constructive way, with the intention and attitude that you are building the relationship, it will improve your marriage.

It's always best to let your spouse know what your intention is. Choose an appropriate time, and using language that your partner will connect with, say something like this: "We are going to be together for the rest of our lives. I love you, and I want to keep you forever. I want us to have not just a good relationship, but a great one. I want us to constantly improve our marriage so that it will be happy and harmonious. I need your help to do this; we are partners. Can we talk about some things that I think need our attention?"

It's also necessary to have the courage to look at yourself to see what *you* are doing that is harmful to the relationship. For example, when you communicate indirectly, your spouse may not get what you are trying to say. For example, if you say, "I'm having trouble doing my work—the TV is so loud," your spouse may or may not get the hint. Instead say, "Would you please lower the TV? I'm trying to work. Thank you."

Express yourself in a direct and appropriate manner regarding anything that you feel is out of balance. If your spouse is constantly complaining, you can gently say, "I feel like I am being a bad spouse because you complain about things. It would be better if you would just say specifically what is making you unhappy, so that I can do something about it."

Or if your spouse constantly criticizes you, try saying, "It makes me feel bad when you criticize me and use that condescending tone. You need to know that it damages our relationship. It would be better if you would tell me directly what's disturbing you."

Sandy and Jake

Sandy complained that Jake constantly said little things to her that put her down—and her self-esteem was suffering. She felt that Jake did not value her as a person or as his wife.

I suggested to Sandy that she stand up for herself and speak to Jake in a constructive way, but with a firm attitude of "No more."

First we changed Sandy's thoughts about herself to bolster her self-esteem. She realized that when she was a child, her mother would put her down, which influenced her thinking about herself. Then we changed her negative thinking about Jake; she admitted that she may have exaggerated his flaws in her mind. We then focused on Jake's positive attributes. She knew that he loved her, so I helped her understand that his put-downs were most likely not intentional and may just have been an unconscious bad habit or the result of insecurity.

I suggested that Sandy say to Jake in an informative way, "I know that you don't realize this, but very often when you speak to me, you say little things that put me down. This hurts me, and it hurts our relationship. I know that you wouldn't do that intentionally, so I would appreciate you becoming more aware of the things that you say to me. I am a woman; I have sensitive feelings. I need to know that you think of me in a good way. So would you please be more conscious of what you are saying to me? Do you understand what I'm trying to tell you?"

I also mentioned to Sandy that it would be a good idea to give Jake an example of something that he had said that made her feel bad about herself. I encouraged her to display understanding rather than anger when she spoke to Jake, so that his reaction would more likely be a positive one.

It turned out that Jake wasn't aware of his bad habit of putting Sandy down, and he vowed to be more aware of how he spoke to her. Sandy and Jake improved themselves and their relationship through this challenge.

Even if you are afraid of your spouse's reaction, if your self-esteem is suffering because of his or her words or behavior, you must stand up for yourself in a way that preserves and strengthens your dignity, your spouse's dignity, and your marriage. If your spouse reacts negatively for whatever reason, then say calmly, "Let's finish this another time when we can discuss this constructively."

When you're trying to improve your self-esteem, it's best not to compare yourself to anyone else.

To make the point, consider the aspiring basketball player who constantly compares himself to Kobe Bryant, one of the greatest basketball players of all time. He may eventually feel like a failure, or may not feel good enough even to play basketball. It's more productive to simply admire Kobe and strive to emulate some of his techniques.

If we compare ourselves to Hollywood actors or supermodels, our self-esteem may suffer. In real life, these people do not wake up in the morning looking like they do in the movies or photographs.

There are many things you can do to increase your self-esteem. Here are a few:

- Read *The Assertive Option: Your Rights and Responsibilities.* Authors Patricia Jakubowski and Arthur Lange offer excellent advice.
- Visit *Dreamality.com.* Founders Arjang and Nicole Zendehdel lead coaching seminars for people who want to improve their self-esteem and create success in life.
- Free yourself from any addictions. Your self-confidence increases when you feel you have some control over your life.
- Read Dale Carnegie's classic book, *How to Win Friends and Influence People,* and visit *DaleCarnegie.com.*

Acquiring self-knowledge always increases self-esteem. When you realize your limits, skills, and talents, you have more confidence in your actions.

Learning your personality type through one of the many personality analysis programs is another way to improve self-esteem. Here are a few:

- *RochelConsulting.com* will help you figure out your and your spouse's personality type.
- Myers-Briggs Personality Typing (*MyersBriggs.org*) is very helpful.
- The Enneagram System is explained in *Bringing Out the Best in Yourself at Work: How to Use the Enneagram System for Success* by Ginger Latip-Bogda, PhD. The author clarifies how our own and other people's actions are influenced by our different personalities.
- David Keirsy (*Keirsy.com*) also has an excellent system for exploring personality types.

A very easy way to increase your self-esteem is by doing good deeds and helping others, including your spouse. When you do a good deed, you'll help yourself too, because you'll feel so good about what you did.

When you are working at a job that is inspiring and fulfilling, your self-esteem increases. In his book *Stressed In*, Robert Bornstein, DO, offers a thought process that can help you discern your passion or skills regarding a career. Dr. Bornstein suggests not using financial gain as a guide; instead he recommends making a list of things that you feel passionate about. He says that these will be the best areas in which to seek employment or create your own business.

Another way to increase your self-esteem is to become healthy and fit. Choosing a more nutritious diet and starting an exercise program makes everyone feel good. An excellent website with great guidance is *WellnessWithDrNikki.com*.

Mirror, Mirror On Your Spouse

A great way to learn about yourself is to observe the "mirror effect."

> *Esoteric teachings say that when someone has a character trait that really irritates you, you should look within yourself—you will see it there too.*

It irritates us because we unknowingly recognize it; subconsciously, we know that trait is within us. If we did not recognize it, it would not cause irritation.

Here's an illustration: if you are annoyed that your spouse has a messy area in the home, you may find an area in your life that is also disorganized, whether it's emotional turmoil or an untidy car.

You may deny to yourself that the trait is also within you. It may take a while, but if you keep looking within, you will eventually find it. The trait may be disguised; it may not look the same as it does in the other person, or it may be buried very deep. But with continuous, gentle digging, you can find it and weed it out. This is part of the refinement process, of growth.

Be motivated and willing to overcome your imperfections and enhance your positive attributes; doing so is for *your* benefit.

For example, if you recognize that you are excessively timid, you must strive to be more assertive. If you are aware that you are excessively aggressive, you must strive to have more compassion.

Role Models

Our parents are good role models. In them, we can see what behaviors we like and want to emulate, or what dispositions we don't like and do not want to display in our lives.

We can also observe other people, and when we see what we think is a good quality, we can incorporate that quality into our own ways.

Observing negative traits in others is just as important as observing positive ones, because then we can make sure that we never incorporate those into our own character.

The best role models are people who believe in peace and in loving others as we love ourselves, such as the Rebbe, Mother Teresa, or your wonderful neighbor who always seems to be helping others. Sometimes heroes can be living right next door to you.

Desire to Change

*To change your life, you must become
aware of your unconscious desires.*

A hidden desire may attract into your life people and events that you don't particularly want.

I know a woman who has a life filled with constant drama and stress. She has expressed to me on many occasions that she would love to have peace and harmony in her life, yet stressful situations often find their way to her. When her life does become peaceful, suddenly a "traumatic" event occurs and drama runs amok. Knowing what I know about this woman, I've concluded that she is a drama queen who seems to thrive with all that chaos in her life. After a crisis, she loves the sympathy she receives from her family and friends. It's also clear to me that her desire for drama is hidden from her own consciousness. Even though she says she longs for peace and harmony, she seems to have a subconscious desire for drama, for being victimized and receiving sympathy in the aftermath. It interests me to observe that she is married to the world's biggest drama king.

Notice what factors are dominant in your life (as drama, victimization, and sympathy are with the woman in the above paragraph). Evaluate your desires in order to discern the path you are on. If you long for peace, ask yourself, *Am I seeking peace? Am I doing things that will bring peace into my life?*

If there is constant arguing and fighting in your marital relationship and you want to change it, the two of you must consciously desire to be peaceful and harmonious. Once you have made that decision, taking action to bring peace into your lives, as well as discontinuing actions that cause discord, will enable harmony to prevail.

To transform your life, it's not necessary to uproot yourself by changing your home, your country, your job, or your spouse. In fact, it's always best to remain exactly where you are, in the same home or job and with the same life partner, and do your "work" from there. The exception is if your well-being or life is at risk.

When you uproot yourself, it may feel exciting and different in the beginning. But eventually things will seem very similar to how they originally were, because the growth that you must experience is still there, waiting for you.

To make a lasting difference, you must determine what it is about yourself that you want to transform, and then take one small step at a time and practice that on a consistent basis. If you try to make too big a change too quickly, you may become overwhelmed and give up.

Change will not happen on its own. When you have the sincere intention and take action to make the transformation persistently and consistently, it **will** happen.

Purpose

You *are* your brother's and sister's keeper.

We must be lamplighters to all those who need help, so that we can bring an era of love and peace into this world. What a boost to our self-esteem!

Ultimately

Be willing to go through the process of refining yourself. When you have some control over your life, the direction of your path will be so much more fulfilling and exciting. You were given the abilities of thought, speech, and action, and so you must learn how to refine yourself through these gifts.

Happiness does not depend on environment; it comes from within. Choose to be happy, and find ways to fulfill that desire. Invite happiness into your life by being gentle and kind and keeping your thoughts and attitudes positive. The more you work to improve yourself, the better and happier your life will be.

The people around you are affected by how you choose to live your life. Your life mate is the one who will be impacted the most.

If you grow and refine yourself, you can live the life you were meant to live. You can measure your growth by how loving, patient, kind, compassionate, and understanding you are with others, especially your partner in life.

To a large extent, you are responsible for creating
your own future through the choices you make.

Now that you know your "self," the next chapter will help you get to know your other important half.

Key Points

- By improving yourself first, you will automatically transform your relationship.
- Your marriage will not improve without your making the effort.
- Change negative thinking habits to positive ones.
- *How* you communicate is extremely important.
- You must express your needs to your spouse.
- Your spouse is your mirror.
- Make the *choice* to be happy.

Chapter 3

Know Your Partner

There he is, working on his project, but his relentless desire to make her happy is distracting him. She is the apple of his eye, the love of his life, the center of his universe. He smiles as he remembers the fragrance of her soft, flowing hair. His heart beats louder, as though it might leap out of his chest and run into her warm, loving arms. Just the thought of her beautiful essence makes goose bumps run up and down his arms. He has an overwhelming urge to seek her out and whisper in her ear how much he loves her. He rushes to find her.

♥

No matter what we do or who we are, our lives are interdependent with those of other people, primarily the people we live with. If we hope to have peace and harmony in the home, it's crucial to get to know our life mate in order to avoid misunderstandings and miscommunications.

It's important to learn what makes your life partner happy, and do more of that—this strengthens the relationship. It's also vital to know what makes your spouse upset, and avoid that. Imagine if your life mate kept doing something that was hurtful or distasteful to you, something that stirred up your negative emotions. Would your love for your partner grow? Probably not. You must therefore do your best to eliminate any actions your partner finds offensive.

A key to successful marriage is realizing
that if you want to receive love from your
spouse, then you must be loving too.

That may seem obvious, but many people expect to be loved by their partner even though they don't behave in a loving manner.

Getting to Know You

During the first year of marriage, we discover that we are living with a person who thinks and behaves differently than we do. We often expect our spouse to be like us and desire the same things we do.

Getting to know your partner helps you realize that you are two separate, unique individuals with different perceptions and dreams, different likes and dislikes, and different ways of doing things. With this knowledge, you can better understand your spouse and the reasons behind the things he or she says and does.

If you are not thus enlightened, miscommunications can happen, causing discord in your relationship.

It's also important to express your needs to your partner— your likes and dislikes, your preferences, the way you want to be loved, and so on. This can be done whenever the occasion arises.

A friend of mine once complained to me because her husband had given her a vacuum cleaner for her birthday. I mentioned to her that he obviously had no clue what kind of birthday present would make her happy, and this was an opportunity to help him learn something about her.

I suggested that she inform her husband in a loving way that she really appreciated him remembering her birthday and going to the effort of buying her a gift, and that she would appreciate it even more if she received a personal gift, such as jewelry or clothing or even a gift card from her favorite store. Her husband was relieved when she told him, because he had no idea what to get for her birthdays.

Appreciating Your Spouse

In reality, if husbands and wives were exactly alike, marriage would probably be a mundane existence. It's our differences that stimulate our interest in each other and keep it alive. We can also admire and appreciate our spouse's uniqueness rather than viewing it negatively.

Brittany and Justin

Brittany complained to me that when she and Justin had to make an important decision together, she had to wait hours, sometimes days, because he wanted to do "so much" research. She said that she could make a decision in a relatively short amount of time.

I helped Brittany understand that Justin was the analytical type. He needed to do research so that he could feel comfortable with his decisions. I asked her if she felt confident in the decisions Justin made, and she realized that she indeed did. I mentioned that perhaps this could be a lesson in patience for her. (She admitted that she was not a very patient person—a negative tendency that she needed to refine.) I pointed out that she could appreciate this difference between them—both their ways were valid; one way was not better than the other—and practice her patience while she was waiting for him to finish his research.

Their Needs

Some people are not skilled at expressing themselves. If that's the case with your spouse, the best and most obvious way to get to know him or her might be through observation and asking questions.

For example, ask about his or her childhood: school experiences, relationship with parents and siblings, best and worst times. Ask about his or her favorite things, inhibitions, insecurities, fears, dreams, like and dislikes, worries and anxieties. What makes him or her feel loved and happy? You can also ask if his or her needs are being met.

Loving Their Way

Most people give love according to how *they* would like to receive love. Many couples make this mistake and struggle for years, thinking there is nothing they can do to please each other.

What pleases you and makes you feel loved may not create the same reaction in your partner. You need to love your spouse in a way that he or she accepts and appreciates. Ask your life mate what makes him or her feel loved, instead of presuming that it is the same thing that you desire.

For example, when selecting a gift for your spouse, keep in mind that he or she might not appreciate the kind of gift that you would like to receive. Focus on something he or she would like, even if you can't relate to that particular item.

Many men feel loved when their wife cooks for them. That's where the expression "The way to a man's heart is through his stomach" comes from.

Many women today don't cook, and when they do, their husbands don't like their cooking. A woman whose husband criticizes or complains about her cooking may become reluctant to make him meals. It would be more productive for him to gently guide her in preparing food in a way that he would enjoy.

Today, there are cooking schools, cooking shows on TV, and cooking information on the Internet. A wife can ask her husband about every meal—what he likes and doesn't like, what herbs and spices he prefers. She shouldn't be afraid to experiment. With persistence, her husband will come to enjoy her food, and that will make her feel good too.

Most women feel loved when they feel listened to. This makes a woman feel validated and important to her husband.

In order for couples to do loving things for each other, they must express their needs and help each other understand those needs. Your spouse may not know what makes you feel special.

Doing things that make your spouse feel special to you, even though that same thing would not cause you to feel the same way, is vital to your marriage.

Their Body Language

You must observe your spouse's tone of voice and body language.

A facial expression can sometimes tell more about what a person is feeling than his or her words. (As the saying goes, a picture is worth a thousand words.) Any part of the body can be used for self-expression, consciously or unconsciously.

Sandi and Mitch

Sandi said that her husband, Mitch, had a very short attention span and would become disconnected and upset during some of their conversations. I suggested that Sandi observe his body language for clues that he was starting to disconnect.

She noticed that during certain conversations, his foot would give an involuntary twitch, and at that point his eyes would become vacant. If she continued with the conversation, he would become upset. Now Sandi knows how to avoid an upsetting moment by observing her husband's subtle body language.

Changing Our Spouse's Habits

It's very important to ask your spouse to stop doing things you consider destructive to your relationship. Realize that it's equally detrimental to keep it to yourself and simply hope that one day your partner will stop doing these destructive things. He or she may not be aware of the damage those actions are causing.

What seems harmful to you may not seem destructive to your spouse; therefore, you must request, in an undemanding manner, that he or she discontinue doing it.

Linda and Don

Linda explained that her husband, Don, was in the habit of requesting something from her in a demanding tone and with an attitude that said, "I want it done *now.*"

I suggested to Linda that she patiently tell him, "You may not realize this, but when you request something from me, your tone is very demanding, and you seem to have the attitude that you want me to drop whatever I'm doing and attend to your needs immediately. I can appreciate that. What I need you to understand is that I am a person also. I've got things I need to get done, and sometimes I have to finish what I'm doing before I can attend to your needs. So when you request something from me, realize that I may not be able to just drop what I am doing. As soon as I can, I will attend to your needs."

I also pointed out that she could simply say, "Give me five minutes, please," or, if it wasn't urgent, "I'll take care of that when I'm finished with what I'm doing."

Once you have spoken to your spouse about discontinuing whatever bad habit you think is harmful to your relationship, be patient. Your partner can't push a button and instantly delete that bad habit. It takes time and effort to eliminate old habits, especially if they have been repeated over a long period of time. Your life mate may need a gentle reminder or two ... or three.

It's to your advantage to be fair and reasonable so that any future requests will not be met with apprehension. Realize that your partner is making the adjustments for your sake. If you hadn't requested them, your spouse may not have even thought about making any changes.

Sometimes your life partner may agree to eliminate a habit but may also want to compromise. Be willing to cooperate.

When your spouse makes a request, being cooperative and quick to make the change demonstrates to him or her how much you care, and it also sets a precedent.

If your spouse asks you to change and you don't make any effort to do so, he or she may not be as cooperative with your next request. You must be sure to set an example. You cannot expect your life mate to transform his or her habits if you are not prepared to do the same.

What's Important

Learning what's important to your loved one will strengthen your relationship.

Valerie and Gabe

Valerie explained that Gabe was so intent on fixing the filing cabinet they shared that he didn't pay attention to how he took the files out of the cabinet so he could repair it. As a result, Valerie's files got all mixed up. These were her personal files, and they were important to her. This caused tension between them.

Your spouse is important to you, so whatever is important to him or her must be respected.

Their Language

Getting to know your spouse's personal language (see chapter 4) can prevent the majority of misunderstandings and miscommunications between you.

Acceptance

This may seem obvious, but it's important to realize that your spouse is a human being just like you, and that no human is perfect. If we were all born perfect, there would be nothing for us to strive for.

It would be unreasonable to expect your partner to be perfect (exactly how you would like him or her to be in every respect), since you are not perfect either. Life is a learning process for everyone; having patience with each other prevents disharmony. There are some habits or ways about your spouse that you'll simply need to accept. You too have quirks and traits that your partner accepts.

Sharona and Andy

Sharona lamented that she had "post-traumatic stress syndrome" from Andy's loud sneezes.

I pointed out that the best thing to do was accept that this was one of Andy's ways and not let it disturb the harmony in their marriage. However, she could ask Andy to try and warn her before he sneezed so that she could protect her ears. She did, and Andy complied—most of the time.

It's vital not to judge, criticize, or belittle your spouse's thoughts, feelings, or ways that differ from yours. Your spouse has a right to feel and think the way he or she does, even if you don't agree with it. Acceptance builds trust in your relationship.

To accept your spouse's different ways, come to the realization that it's okay for him or her to be different from you. Everyone is unique, which makes everyone's thinking different from everyone else's.

It's also important to emphasize that both of you can be right even when you don't agree.

You Turn Me On

It's a good idea to ask your spouse if there is anything you do that is offensive. The less you do to turn off your life mate, the better. After all, when the intention is to spend a lifetime together, it's more fun to spend it with someone who is exciting to you.

Getting to know your spouse helps prevent misunderstandings and helps you accept and understand his or her ways that are different from yours. As a result, you'll strengthen your bond and build your relationship.

Key Points

- Getting to know your spouse prevents disharmony.
- You must not expect your partner to be like you.
- Appreciate and accept your differences, and don't allow them to turn into arguments.
- Love your spouse the way he or she would like to be loved, not the way *you* prefer.
- Ask your life partner to change habits that you feel are destructive to your relationship.
- Be cooperative when your spouse requests a change from you.
- Try to eliminate any habit that offends or turns off your life mate.

Chapter 4

The Differences

They find each other and she melts into his chest, feeling the strength of his masculine arms around her. He inhales her. The warmth of her feminine essence makes him feel euphoric. She giggles with exotic pleasure. The flurry of energy between them ignites into a burst of breathtaking mutual passion. As she gazes into his eyes, they twinkle with exuberant adoration. He bends his head down to her ear and expresses his undying love for her. She melts even further into him.

♥

Male and female energies are opposites. Opposites can attract, and they can also challenge each other. Within each energy are forces that allow for a harmonious connection despite the differences.

Understanding Differences and Equality

A key to successful marriage is realizing
that men and women are opposites.

Men and women have both male and female energies within them. Obviously, a man has more of the male energy within him and a woman has more of the female energy within her.

Many men and women complain that they do not understand each other. We tend to assume that people of the opposite gender are like us, since we are all part of the human race. However, the differences between men and women can be compared to the "yin and yang" concept. Men and women have brains that are wired differently, they communicate in distinctly different ways, and their physical bodies are obviously dissimilar. Once they understand these differences, men and women can be more accepting of each other.

If men and women were exactly alike, life together would be very predictable. As intelligent human beings, we need the stimulation and excitement the opposite gender provides. It's also important to realize that the differences between men and women help them grow. Accepting these differences strengthens a marriage, and not being accepting creates dissension.

Each gender has unique qualities to bring to a relationship, and each plays a role in bringing out the essence of the other. It is important for life partners to focus not on the contrast, but on becoming greater as a couple than they are as individuals.

Men and women complement each other in areas where one or the other lacks. Each energy, male and female, depends upon the other to bring balance into the family unit. In other words, men and women have different but equally important roles in their marriage and in the world.

Let's take a look at some of these differences.

The Feminine

The wife bears the majority of the powerful feminine energy in the marriage and has different responsibilities in the relationship than her husband.

In general, women are more detail oriented. A woman is good at multitasking. Her emotions are involved with everything she does. She is cooperative yet cautious at the same time. Her nature is geared toward family and relationships. She has innate qualities made for creating the home environment—she is nurturing, patient, kind, and gentle, perfect qualities for raising children and preparing them for their future, and for taking care of her husband with healthy foods, supporting him, and boosting his self-esteem so that he is powerful in the world. These qualities are also suitable for creating a peaceful and harmonious marriage.

A woman uses her speech for building bonds and relationships. She includes many people within her circle. At work, her qualities can facilitate collaboration and peaceable communications.

When she's upset, she needs to talk and may become emotional. When she's stressed, she may become anxious, lack energy, or want to cry. She may be indirect about her feelings. When she is unhappy with her partner, she may feel disappointed.

Women's bodies have less muscle than men's.

The Masculine

The husband bears the majority of the powerful masculine energy in the marriage and has different responsibilities in the relationship than his wife.

In general, men are more solution oriented and tend to focus on one issue at a time. Men tend to be competitive and assertive. He uses his speech for relaying facts and information. He may be very direct in his speech and actions.

When he is upset, he may become emotionally detached and may need space and time for himself, retreating into his inner sanctum. When he is unhappy with his partner, he may feel frustrated. When he's stressed, he may suffer from insomnia and feel angry or irritated. He will be less likely than a woman to admit that the stress is affecting him.

The innate qualities of the male energy are physical strength, protectiveness, and the ability to become emotionally detached. These attributes are perfect for someone who must go out into the world, be the primary provider, and protect and sustain his loved ones.

Men's bodies have more muscle than women's.

The Roles

Women, with their feminine energy, are mostly
responsible for influencing the tone in the home.

Of course, both spouses must be accountable for harmony in their home, but for the most part the woman takes the lead. If she is negative in her thoughts toward her spouse, her actions will be contrary, the home environment will be disharmonious, and thus the marriage will be contentious.

The feminine energy is very powerful. It has the ability to subdue the male warrior energy.

For example, applying her feminine qualities, she can freshen up her hair and makeup before her husband arrives home and then greet him with love and affection. Her femininity has the power to soothe and calm his warrior energy.

She can then practice her patience by allowing him fifteen to thirty minutes to play with the kids or the dog, or just be alone, before she talks about her day. This will allow him to further disperse any aggressiveness from being out in the world. After unwinding, he may be a better, more patient listener.

If she immediately starts complaining about her day or accuses him of being late or not returning her calls, he may perceive that their home is not a warm, welcoming, or loving environment. After a long day out in the world, he may not look forward to going home.

A wife can make their abode a place where he feels welcome and loved as soon as he walks in the door. A very important step in this process is looking happy to see him. That will set the tone for the rest of the evening and through the next morning until he leaves for work.

If she uses her feminine energy appropriately to send her husband off to work, it will carry him through the day. She can make herself look attractive before he leaves so that he will have a great image of her in his mind. If she sends him off with love, hugs, and kisses, she will uplift him. He will most likely have a good day, and his self-esteem will be empowered. Consequently, he will be a better provider for the family.

Today, both spouses work in many families, so whoever arrives home first will be the one to greet his or her partner in the appropriate way. If the husband arrives first and has had time alone, the wife can talk about her day when she gets home.

A man, with his powerful masculine energy, is mostly responsible for bringing security (financial, physical, and emotional) to his family, which depends on him for protection and sustenance.

If a man's thoughts are not focused on his family and his career, he may not be able to fulfill his mission in life. He must not allow himself to be distracted.

We are all human, and we all have our "off" days, or days when we're feeling "not so loving," but making a special effort fortifies the marital relationship.

In countries where women are abused and oppressed, the men are noticeably more harsh and violent. The female energy, which is more gentle and nurturing, is subjugated in these areas, and obviously the male energy is out of balance. This imbalance affects not only those countries, but the whole world.

Say What?

Adding to the confusion is the fact that each partner in a marriage has his or her own "language." Even though the person you are talking to speaks the same language that you do, there may still be misunderstandings and miscommunications between you.

Here are some of the reasons for this:

- Words mean different things to different people.
- Each family has its own way of communicating.
- Some people are more visual, some are more auditory, and some are more feeling oriented.

- Some people are hypersensitive and some are non-sensitive.
- Some people are detail oriented while others see the "big picture."
- Some people are introverts while others are extroverts.

If a couple is not aware of this "language" difference, it may create discord in their marriage.

Let's take the word *ignorant*. To one person, the word may mean exactly what it says in the dictionary ("lacking knowledge, unaware, uninformed"), but to another it may have a very negative connotation, such as "stupid" or "dumb."

Connie and Brody

Connie told me that her husband, Brody, would always become angrier when she asked him, "Why are you so angry?" He would furiously respond, "I'm not angry!" I suggested that she ask him what *he* would call his animated display.

To her surprise, Brody said that he was just "frustrated." To him he was only frustrated; to her he was angry. Now when Connie asks Brody, "Why are you so frustrated?" he responds with an answer instead of becoming more upset.

A conversation is like a dance. One partner may know how to tango while the other knows how to waltz. They are both dances, but they are very different. A couple can't dance together if one person is doing the tango and the other is waltzing. In order to harmonize, they need to learn each other's moves—or they can both learn a new style together, like jazz. A professional dancer knows all dancing styles. In the same way, a skilled communicator is able to communicate successfully with anyone.

Phil and Beth

Phil told me that he and Beth would help each other get off the computer when it got late. As he explained it, he would remind

Beth how late it was by asking her, "What time is it?" Then Beth would understand that it was time to put the computer to sleep.

However, Beth complained that whenever she reminded Phil of the time, he would thank her for reminding him but then remain on the computer. She would have to remind him two or three times. She was frustrated because Phil kept urging her to give him a reminder. I suggested to Beth that she try using his language, saying, "What time is it?" instead of what she usually said, which was "It's getting late."

The next time Beth used Phil's words to remind him that it was late, he got off the computer within five minutes. When she spoke his language, he immediately connected to what she was saying.

Becoming upset when your spouse misunderstands you only adds to the dilemma. Instead, try a different way of expressing yourself, making sure that your partner comprehends exactly what you are trying to say.

If your spouse says something that seems offensive, make sure that you understood what was being expressed, and avoid becoming instantly upset. You could ask, "Is this what you meant?" and then repeat back in your own words what you think you heard.

The most important thing to realize is that your spouse did not intend to offend or hurt you.

If you have trouble figuring out your life mate's language, visit *RochelConsulting.com* for excellent guidance.

Emotions and Needs

Men and women have different needs too—as if there weren't enough differences to deal with!

Generally, a woman needs to talk about the details, and she needs her husband to listen. This helps her clarify her thinking. If women remembered that it's usually not in a man's nature to listen to the details, they would keep their conversations short and to the point. If they did this, their husbands would most likely pay attention. It's in a woman's nature to listen to the details, so girlfriends are a necessity for her.

If men remembered that a woman needs to be heard out, they would be patient and *listen* to their wives. Women should also realize that when they share their problems with their husbands, he will believe they are seeking advice on how to fix those problems, and it is in his nature to help them do so.

A husband needs to compliment his wife. It's a subliminal assurance that his eyes are only on her. She needs to feel loved, validated, cared for, and desired by him—more assurance.

She needs her husband to treat her gently, as though she's a delicate flower. She will then respond to him in a loving and nurturing way. If he treats her harshly or does not validate her importance in the marriage, she will respond to him in a sharp way, like a rose with thorns.

Generally, men prefer conversations that are direct and to the point. Most men need time alone to sort out their problems. If they can't, then they seek help.

A man needs to feel respected as the head of his household. He needs to feel competent and needs to know that his spouse trusts him to provide. He needs to feel like her hero. He needs to be appreciated for the things he does for her. If she does not show appreciation, he may lose interest.

For the most part, there is a very big difference between a man's emotional makeup and a woman's. To help you understand this, think of a man's emotions as one person riding one horse, and a woman's emotions as one person managing a team of a dozen horses—much harder to manage than just one horse!

A woman may fall much more deeply in love than a man because of her complex and abundant emotions. She will also experience a much broader range of emotional ups and downs than a man. When she is upset, she has a deluge of emotions to deal with. When there is turmoil in a marriage, the woman will suffer more than the man.

Her husband can help her manage her emotions by not reacting to her distress. When he remains calm and confident, he influences her to feel soothed and comforted.

Full Potential

Because of their differences, couples have the ability to bring out each other's latent talents and skills so that they can reach their full potential.

Nora and Don

Don was overwhelmed by Nora's constant complaints about her work at a drug rehabilitation facility. She knew that this was where she wanted to work, but she did not feel totally comfortable with what she was doing. I informed Don that he had the ability to bring out Nora's hidden talents. Instead of becoming frustrated with her, he could try making suggestions.

Don came up with the idea that Nora should try the job placement department in the drug rehabilitation facility, since she had previously worked as a hiring agent for a large corporation. Nora liked the suggestion and applied for a transfer. She blossomed in her new job, and Don hasn't heard a complaint since.

Just Friends?

Some married people have an office "spouse" or "friend"—a coworker of the opposite sex with whom they talk about everything, including their marriage. They eat lunch together and might spend time together after work too. Even though neither person may have initially intended to become physically close, their words and actions may be misconstrued as sexual, which could ultimately lead to adultery. The fact is, their time, energy, and emotions are being invested in each other instead of their life partners and their marriages. Many people don't realize the harm in this situation, which drains both people's marriages of the vital emotional energy that they need for nourishment and growth.

Relationships outside of marriage with the opposite sex must be restricted. For example, a work relationship must be confined to mostly work matters.

Having a work "friend" of the opposite sex can create competition between your spouse and your friend. You may start comparing your friend to your partner. Remember that every time you see your friend, he or she has gotten spruced up to look good. When you see your spouse first thing in the morning, he or she may not look as good as your friend does spruced up.

You can't know what "friends" like these are really like, although you might think you know. They may be irresponsible or insensitive in some other area of their lives that you are not aware of, or they could be the complete opposite of what you may have thought about them. Comparing your spouse to only the fraction that you know about your friend could cause you to begin viewing your life partner in a negative light. For example, you may admire your friend's sense of adventure, and suddenly your spouse, who may be a little conservative (a quality that wasn't noticeable before), may appear boring. Making comparisons may cause unfair judgment of your life partner.

Marlee and Jeff

Marlee and Jeff were married for seven years. Jeff absolutely adored Marlee and did everything he could to make her happy. The challenge in their relationship was that Jeff was not a very communicative person, while Marlee was the opposite—she craved conversation. One day a new neighbor, Josh, moved into the house across the street. He was single and looking to make friends in the neighborhood. As Marlee got to know him, she realized that he liked to make conversation. Marlee was thrilled to have a "friend" who liked to converse. At first, their friendship seemed innocent, but Marlee was focusing more and more of her attention on Josh, who gladly accepted it.

Two months later, Marlee told Jeff that she found him boring (having compared Jeff's communication abilities to Josh's) and that she wanted to be with her new friend. Jeff and Marlee did not have children, so she left that very same day. Jeff was devastated; he'd had no idea that Marlee was so unhappy in their relationship. Marlee and Josh moved out of the neighborhood soon afterward.

After just a few months of living together, Marlee awoke to the fact that Josh was no longer "into" her. She experienced one of his negative tendencies one day when he lashed out at her and told her not to speak (how ironic!). He told her he was done and wanted her to move out—now! Marlee went back to Jeff to see if she could reconcile with him. Even though Jeff still adored her, he no longer trusted her with his heart; he still felt wounded. He did not think that reconciliation was a good idea. Marlee now lives alone. She misses Jeff and is extremely regretful, depressed, and lonely.

To remedy her need for conversation, Marlee could have found and made female friends by joining the local community center or a book club. She could have helped Jeff learn to communicate better, and this may have aided in resolving one of Jeff's negative tendencies (one that Marlee was initially unconsciously attracted to). In helping Jeff refine one of his imperfections, Marlee would have refined herself in the process, thereby nourishing and strengthening their relationship.

Caught in a Web

In recent years, there have been many divorces because of a spouse having a "friend" on the Internet/social media. Internet infidelity! Usually the spouse did not have any physical contact with the other person, and sometimes he or she didn't even know what the "friend" looked like, yet the online relationship still ruined the marriage. That's virtual cheating!

Some people fall in love with a photograph or the words in an e-mail. Photographs and words can be very misleading. I have heard many stories about couples who divorced because of a virtual affair, and then the "friend" turned out not even to be the person in the photograph.

Some people use the Internet or social media to supplement their lives. If you are not careful, you could get caught in that web. I once heard of a man who had two thousand friends on Facebook, but when he passed away, not one single friend showed up at his funeral.

Couples must always remember that no computer activity is more important than their marriage.

Watch Out

Couples should also be aware that there are some single people who, for their own reasons, find married people very attractive. These men and women purposely pursue married people and attempt to seduce them away from their families. They simply don't care; they want what they want, and they don't give a second thought to the fact that they will be destroying a family. These people justify their behavior by saying that they could not have seduced the married person if his or her relationship wasn't already coming to an end.

Extramarital affairs don't just happen; the unfaithful spouse knows when he or she is giving in. The best defense against that kind of weakness is to immediately remove yourself from the temptation and avoid it in the future.

We have seen the consequences of infidelity throughout history—families devastated—yet people are still willing to take the risk for the novelty of someone new and different, or because they were flattered that someone paid special attention to them.

You must be loyal and faithful to your spouse, even in your thoughts.

There will always be other people who seem better than your life partner in one way or another. But it's worth remembering that you are seeing only a small slice of that new person's life, not the whole. Nobody is perfect, even though your fantasies may make that person seem perfect in your eyes. Just like everyone else, your new "friend" has negative tendencies too; you just don't know what they are yet because they have not been revealed to you. Who knows, maybe your friend would not accept your imperfections—like what happened to Marlee.

You can't compare fantasy to reality. In reality, you know only about one percent of who this "friend" is; the rest, 99 percent, is just fabrication. You must not run with a figment of your imagination; the reality may turn out to be the opposite of what you thought.

Your spouse is reality—the person who loves *you*, who wants to spend his or her life with *you* and cares about *your* well-being, *despite* your shortcomings.

If you feel that something is lacking in your marriage, having a friend of the opposite gender will not fill in what's missing; ultimately it will make things worse.

If you are the one with the "friend," consider asking yourself, *How would I feel if my life mate had a special friend and was spending time and energy with that person?* If instead you were to invest all that time and energy in your marriage, your relationship with your spouse would dramatically improve.

*If your manner of connecting to your partner
is not working, keep trying to find new and
different ways that will create a stronger
and more fulfilling bond between you.*

We Are In It Together

Ultimately, husband and wife are equally accountable for the success or failure of their marriage. When both partners make the effort to bring their respective qualities to the relationship in a positive way, they will build the marriage and create a beautiful, harmonious, and loving future together.

Key Points

- Men and women are opposites and should not expect to be alike.
- Men and women, with their different roles, are equally important in their marriage.
- Don't focus on your differences; rather, focus on becoming greater by being united.
- Being accepting fortifies your relationship.
- The wife is primarily responsible for setting the tone in the home.
- The husband is primarily responsible for the physical, emotional, and financial security of his family.
- If a man's focus is distracted from his family and his career, he may not be able to fulfill his mission in life.
- Having a "friend" of the opposite gender outside of marriage could potentially put it in jeopardy.
- If you are not careful, you can get caught in an Internet/social media web.
- Constantly find and create new and different ways to connect with your life mate.

Chapter 5

The Mighty Challenge

They're in the living room. He's standing there with his tanned, muscular arms folded, his face turning slightly red with frustration. She has her small, well-kept hands on her shapely hips and a frown on her usually softened brow. Her long hair pulled back tight, she's ready to strike, like a cobra standing tall. Her words are piercing ... and then she remembers: they are from different planets! She moves closer to him and rests her delicate hands on his heaving chest. A warm, knowing smile flashes across her face, and she quickly kisses him on the tip of his nose. He seems startled and puzzled but at the same time relieved. He cautiously smiles at her in return. The storm is over. They embrace, and all is well in their world.

♥

A lifetime commitment with a Sacred Vow is the most exquisitely rewarding journey anyone could undertake. That said, all journeys have bumps in the road. Whenever two people come together in any situation, tension is bound to happen at some point.

A key to successful marriage is realizing that
marriage is a partnership, and that both partners are
accountable for what happens in their relationship.

Challenges are a part of life. Many couples work out their differences and live the kind of married life that they had intended. Some couples hit a rough patch and give up too easily.

The idea is not to get caught up and stuck in the difficult times. Do your best to work them out in an amicable way, because beyond them lies the fulfillment of your dreams.

Disagreements are an indication that you need to make changes in your relationship—for the better. They are not an indication that your marriage is not working or that the spouse you chose is not the right one. Many people divorce prematurely because of these unfortunate misperceptions.

Nowhere in any teaching does it say, "Your soul mate will make you happy *all* the time." as fairy tales would have us believe.

A key to successful marriage is realizing that challenges have a very important purpose: when we overcome them, we grow. When we grow, we become happier, more secure, and more successful.

Your spouse is your partner in your growth, and vice versa. Growth is necessary but sometimes uncomfortable, so you must not blame your life mate for your discomfort.

As I mentioned, tension arises at some point in all relationships. Egos; miscommunications; gender differences; different beliefs, opinions, and preferences; hormone imbalances; diet and health; anger and emotional issues—any kind of human condition has the capacity to create discord.

Ironically, relationships have the potential to grow the most in times of difficulty. When we feel blissful, we naturally do not want to change anything.

The problem lies in the fact that if we don't continually try to improve, the blissfulness eventually degrades.

Equal Partners

Both spouses are equal participants in a marital challenge.

Even if your spouse appears to have created the tension, how you react to it will determine in which direction the relationship will go. Sometimes you might unknowingly say or do something that creates an argument. So you can't point fingers!

Remember the differences between men and women? Men generally switch off their emotions during disagreements and can become very uncaring. Women generally become very emotional and in that way also can become very uncaring. Being aware of how you respond to disharmony can help you navigate a successful outcome.

For example, if a woman realizes that she becomes overemotional during disagreements with her husband, she can focus on being calm. If a man is aware that he switches off his emotions during arguments with his wife, he can focus on being more open. This process will help resolve the tension and restore the relationship.

A good outcome would be one where the challenge is resolved amicably, where both spouses' dignity and self-respect remain intact and the marital bond is strengthened.

Self-Defense

*We are all susceptible to being cruel and unkind
when we think our own interests are at stake.*

When egos are a priority, they create obstacles that prevent an argument from being resolved in a way that is best for both spouses.

We are all brilliant "self"-defense attorneys when it comes to our egos. They can do no wrong. We'll defend our egos with ferocity, eager to lay the blame on the guilty party—our spouse. We'll even build a substantial case in our own mind against the opposing party—our poor spouse! Before we know it, we've also become the judge and jury. By the time our case gets heard, every one of our words and actions have been justified. Our adult temper tantrum and lack of self-control instantly turn into passion and enthusiasm, and we acquit ourselves of all wrongdoing. The blame lies solely with our unsuspecting spouse: guilty as charged.

If you insist on being judge and jury, consider this: before condemning your spouse to life in purgatory, you are obligated to see his or her point of view. A judge must listen to both sides before ruling.

A responsible action to take is to ask yourself, *What is my part in this disagreement?* Acknowledge that in some way your reactions contributed to the problem.

Who's More Important?

Some couples have the challenge of one spouse feeling more important than the other. Perhaps one partner earns more money, or has a better education, a more prestigious job, or better social skills. His or her sense of greater importance may eventually create a relationship that is out of balance.

When one spouse always wants to win, then the other will feel like the loser—and nobody likes losing. When one wants to be right all the time, then the other will always feel wrong. When one partner wants to be more powerful, then the other will feel a loss of self-esteem. This imbalance will undermine the relationship. When there is self-importance on the part of one partner, and the expectation that the other should comply to suit his or her needs, then the other will not feel valued in the marriage—and this will bring dissatisfaction.

Therefore do unto your spouse what you would have him or her do unto you. If you don't like feeling unimportant, realize that your partner may not like it either.

If your life partner has any of the above issues or is very controlling, you can say in a very neutral and informative way, "I am a valid person too, just like you. I have needs, likes, dislikes, opinions, and dreams that may be different from yours, but that doesn't make them wrong or bad or unimportant—just different from yours, and just as valid. And that's okay; that's how it should be. There is room for both of us in this marriage."

Spouses are partners in life, not competitors who must be overcome and conquered. If you love your partner as you love yourself, you'll automatically want to improve to be a better spouse.

When both partners understand that they are equally important in their respective roles and have needs that are equally valid, they will feel respected and valued in their marriage.

And this may sound obvious, but most of us don't think about it: if you hurt your life mate, you will be living with the person you hurt. Even though your partner may forgive you, he or she will remember the hurt caused by your actions, and you will always have the consequences and regret right in front of you.

Part of the marriage journey is being student and teacher for each other, but you also must be kind and gentle with the one with whom you intend to grow old.

It's All in the "How"

Challenges can be stepping-stones to a better relationship, or they can be stumbling blocks.

How both spouses handle the dispute determines whether its outcome is successful or destructive. Arguing is not the problem; it's *how* the argument is handled that causes it to become damaging.

It may be agitating to discuss the issue, but keeping a goal of resolving the dispute in a constructive manner will allow the discussion to become easier.

When the conflict begins veering off into side issues, or there are all kinds of distractions, or your spouse seems disconnected from what you are attempting to express, or the discussion comes to an end but the conflict doesn't feel resolved, there may be an underlying concern on your part or that of your spouse.

If you have checked your thoughts and did not find any unspoken feelings that may be interfering with a resolution, then try saying to your partner, "We seem to be having a problem resolving this disagreement. What do you think the reason is? Is there something disturbing you regarding this issue? What are you *really* feeling and thinking?"

One way you might influence how your spouse handles the conflict is by speaking aloud as though verbalizing your thoughts—saying, for example, "I'm going to remember that I am speaking to the one I love, so I am going to be kind and gentle ..." and then following with your response. When you express your thoughts out loud, you can help guide your spouse into new and better ways.

Here are more examples:

- "We can handle this disagreement in a respectful way."
- "We are in this together; let's be amicable."
- "We make a good partnership; we can be reasonable."
- "Let's remember that we are on the same side."
- "We can be constructive in handling this argument."
- "Let's not make this bigger than what it is."
- "Let's keep things in perspective."
- "Let's remember that our marriage is more important than this dispute."

Challenges in a relationship are both indicators and opportunities.

Indicators

Difficulties indicate that it's time to transition the relationship to a higher level. No relationship remains the same forever; either it grows or it degrades over time. Tension simply means that the couple has not made any recent effort to improve their marriage. The universe is now forcing them to pay attention.

If both partners handle the challenge in a constructive way by remembering that they are communicating with their loved one, they will experience growth and build the relationship.

If they handle it in a contrary way by allowing their egos or negative tendencies to drive their arguments, then they will be tearing down their relationship.

Opportunities

Challenges also present us with the opportunity to measure our growth. We can gauge our growth by how patient, kind, respectful, and understanding we are with our life partner.

Obviously, the more of your true nature you integrate into your personality, the more you have grown and refined yourself. If you have allowed your negative disposition to prevent your growth, you must overcome it. The more you grow, the happier you will become, and the more secure you will be in your marriage.

For Men

Given the differences between men and women, it stands to reason that when your wife is upset, she would feel loved and supported if you would say, "Do you want to talk about it?" Be patient and just listen to her complaints rather than giving her space or trying to fix or minimize her complaints by saying, "It's no big deal." You can also ask, "Would you like my opinion or suggestion?" It will facilitate the dialogue if you recognize that her feelings are valid even though you may not agree with them. Just by being listened to, she will feel supported and cared for. After she's finished talking, she may even say, "Thank you—that was so helpful," even though all you did was listen.

If you're not sure exactly what she needs from you, you could gently say, "I don't understand. What are you are trying to tell me?" If you perceive that she is complaining about you, you could patiently say, "Tell me exactly what it is that you need from me." Since you feel she is complaining about you, your ego may be aroused. At this point, your natural ability to detach from your emotions may kick in. Try to resist this reaction and stay centered and engaged.

When she complains—or nags, as guys like to call it—she is generally not accusing or criticizing, but calling for a change for the better. Remember, she may be communicating indirectly, which is what her "complaining" usually is. Try listening for what she is requesting, or you can guess. ("Is this what you want from me...?")

You can also help her learn how to ask for change in a more direct way rather than complaining. Inform her, "If you want me to understand what you are trying to tell me, then be short and to the point. For example, instead of complaining about the trash piling up, just ask me to take the trash out, and I will gladly do so." (And guys, don't forget to take the trash out if you want her to stop complaining!)

If she needs to talk and you feel that you are not capable of a constructive discussion at that moment, you can say, "Let's talk later because I can't focus right now." Be considerate and don't keep her waiting hours or days; respond in a reasonable amount of time. The longer you wait, the more time she has to imagine the worst.

Remember to be kind and patient; she is learning a new language.

For Women

Given the differences between men and women, it stands to reason that when he is upset, he would feel loved and supported if you would say, "Would you like some time to yourself?" or "Let's talk in an hour." Then be patient by giving him space and time. If he has some time to himself, he will usually come to the conclusion that whatever was bothering him wasn't as big a deal as it appeared to be in the beginning. If he is confronted when he is upset, he may be forced to defend himself or he may totally withdraw.

If he insists on talking when his emotions are hot, don't engage! It is usually because he wants to blow off steam. He is a warrior by nature, and his anger will be directed toward you. Say to him, "No, let's not talk right now because it won't be constructive. Let's talk later," and give him space. Choose a time when he is calm and relaxed, such as after a meal.

You can make tension worse by ignoring him or giving him the silent treatment—this damages the relationship. Respond to him in a reasonable amount of time; don't keep him waiting hours or days.

The most constructive way for you to get your husband's attention and get him to stay in the room to talk about your challenge is to resist the urge to criticize, accuse, blame, shame, make him feel unimportant, or coerce him into doing what you want him to do. If you don't resist that urge, he will start to roll his eyes or disengage. Getting to the point as quickly as possible is what will keep his attention.

Imagine this scenario, for example:

A wife says to her husband, "When I walk into the bathroom and I see the towels on the floor, it always makes me so upset. I feel like I'm your mother picking up after you." At this point, he starts rolling his eyes. "The towels stay wet and they stink, so then I have to wash them more often, and I only have time to do washing twice a week. I feel like I'm slaving after you." By now he has disengaged. "By the time I get home, I'm so tired that I really don't feel like picking up your towels. I've spoken to you about this before, but you never listen. You just don't care—you don't even try." By now he's on another planet. "Can't you just help me and hang them up so that they can dry out?" By this time he just wants to get out of there, and so he says, "Will do!" and makes his exit. But the next time she walks into the bathroom, there are the towels on the floor ... again ... because he could not "hear" what she was saying.

He could not hear her message because 1) there was too much detail for his nature to handle; 2) it sounded like complaining to him; and 3) it was not short and to the point.

If her speech is not short and to the point, he most likely will not respond to her in an appropriate way. To accomplish her goal, she can make her request this way instead: "Will you please hang up the towels when you are done with them so that they can dry out, instead of throwing them on the floor—will you?"

When you have a dilemma and all you want to do is talk about it and not have it "fixed," then you need to tell your husband, "I just want to talk about this—you don't have to fix anything. Please, would you just listen?"

It's important for a woman to know that her husband really does want to make things better for her. If your husband appears not to be listening and tries to give you suggestions, realize that it is his way of being helpful, by creating a solution.

Try very hard not to make him feel like he is always in the wrong. He might get to the point that he thinks, *What have I done wrong now?* Rather, share your ideas, gently guide him, and be a role model. If he feels he is always in the wrong, he may one day feel that he is the wrong one for you.

Remember to be kind and patient; he is learning a new language.

The most obvious time for arguments to take place is in the early evening, after a long day of work and when you are in need of nourishment. It's best to postpone any important discussions for later, after you've changed into comfortable clothes, eaten dinner, and put the kids to bed, or whatever time of day or night you communicate best as a couple.

The Unique Challenge

Each person is a unique individual, and when two individuals come together, it creates a unique relationship. Therefore, every marriage has its own set of unique challenges. Usually, a couple falls very quickly into a pattern of reacting to each other that allows an argument to ensue.

In fact, most couples have more than one such pattern. Discovering them can completely resolve these difficulties or even prevent them by helping the couple reveal their negative traits that need correcting. It also creates a happier and more secure marriage in the long run.

A key to successful marriage is realizing that challenges reveal our negative tendencies that must be transformed.

Leon and Sylvia

Sylvia told me that her husband, Leon, became easily frustrated. She described herself as a compliant person who tried to please everyone. To discover their pattern, we analyzed exactly what happened during their disagreements.

First Leon became frustrated (a negative tendency) about something related, or even unrelated, to Sylvia. Sylvia then became defensive (a negative tendency), and an argument followed.

I suggested to Leon that he needed to learn to take responsibility for his emotions and not blame Sylvia for how he was feeling at the time. He also needed to use his words appropriately.

I pointed out to Sylvia that she could immediately control the direction of the dispute by altering her response to Leon. To discover why she got defensive when Leon showed frustration toward her, I asked her to pay attention to her feelings at that moment. She realized that his behavior felt like a "sudden attack" on her, which made her feel extremely anxious; therefore she couldn't respond in a constructive way.

Once Sylvia uncovered her pattern of communicating with Leon, she could change her response and use her affirmations: *It's okay. He is not attacking me; he is just frustrated. I can be calm. I don't need to be defensive. I can react in a positive way.*

At the same time, her new way of responding made Leon recognize his own negative behavior, which helped him gain self-control. This stopped the tension from becoming destructive.

I mentioned to Sylvia that if she felt anxious and couldn't respond appropriately at that moment, she could simply say, "Let's talk in ten minutes—you seem frustrated right now," which would also direct Leon to behave in a different way as well. It would also give her time to calm her anxiety and think of a constructive response.

Discovering this pattern helped Sylvia and Leon transform the negative tendencies of their personalities that needed refining. They are much happier now, both with themselves and with their marriage.

You can also break a pattern by responding to your spouse in a completely different way than you normally do—that is, by doing or saying something that your spouse hasn't experienced from you before.

Fred and Maya

Fred said that his wife, Maya, had a quick temper. He would react to her temper with anger, and they would end up having a shouting match. Fred decided that this was destructive to their marriage and wanted to change this pattern.

I suggested to Fred that the next time Maya overreacted, he could try something that she had never experienced from him before, such as not responding until she became calm.

The next time Maya became angry, she furiously said to Fred, "Well, aren't you going to say something?" He replied very patiently, "No, I'm waiting for you to calm down." Fred said that at first Maya became even more incensed, but still he kept quiet, looking at her with his "I'm waiting" face. Maya finally realized that he was not going to respond until she controlled her anger, so she said, "Okay, I'll calm down." They were then able to have a reasonable discussion and resolve their disagreement.

During an argument, it is always best to begin sentences with the word *I* or *We* and not with the word *You*. For example, avoid saying, "You never...," or "You always...." It is more constructive to start a sentence with "I feel...." Beginning your sentence with the word *You* can make your spouse feel accused or criticized and immediately become defensive. At that point, the argument will most likely turn destructive.

Always remember that your relationship is more important than any challenge. The tension will pass, but the marriage is for a lifetime.

You must make sure that your spouse knows that he or she matters more to you than your frustrations—and you can do this by not striking out verbally. Instead, say in a neutral way, "What you did made me feel really angry, but I'm willing to give you the benefit of the doubt. I'm going to listen to your side of the story."

Derailment

Practically anything can derail a relationship: even a weird look, a sound, a combative tone, or sarcasm will do it. The sooner the couple communicates to get back on track, the better it is for the relationship. When marital challenges are left to fester, memories become contaminated by emotions and perceptions, and resentments begin to accumulate. Once that happens, it will take more time and effort to realign the marriage.

It's unrealistic to expect a relationship to be harmonious 100 percent of the time, considering the fact that no one is harmonious within him- or herself 100 percent of the time. It's during these down times that a little more work is required of us. The more vigilant we are, the sooner they will pass.

When you feel your spouse is not treating you lovingly, looking at your own attitude first can be revealing. Your partner may be reacting to your negative disposition, which you may not be aware of.

Misunderstandings can happen very easily, especially if you assume that you know what your spouse is thinking. You may think you can read your spouse's mind, but you also could be completely wrong. If his or her words didn't sound loving or kind, you must ask exactly what was intended. You could say,

"That sounded nasty. Did you mean...?" If nothing constructive is accomplished, try saying, "I don't think we are on the same page. Let's take a break and talk later." Become aware of when any discussion turns destructive or if there is a miscommunication—allowing such a pattern to continue can be damaging.

Sometimes both spouses will remain convinced that they are right and the other is wrong. If that's still the case even after each partner has explained his or her point of view, it is best to set aside the disagreement and not pursue an outcome. Driving an issue into the ground just to prove that you were right and your partner was wrong can derail a relationship.

Tension with in-laws can cause derailment too. In most cases, it's best to let family deal with family. In other words, you deal with your family and let your spouse deal with his or her family.

If you constantly take your family's side against your spouse, he or she may eventually feel like an outsider. Family is important, but your life mate is more important. Your spouse is your partner in life, the one you will be spending the rest of your life with.

Sometimes well-meaning family members can prevent your potential growth. You must cut the apron strings and know that your journey is now with your life mate. I've known more than one loving mother who didn't like the way her "baby" was being treated by a spouse and eventually was the influence that caused her "baby's" divorce. A mother will always be a mother, no matter how old her child is, but when that child enters into a journey with a loved one, he or she must evolve in order to grow further.

Over and Over

Most couples have one or two difficulties that keep coming up over and over again, recurring challenges that just can't seem to get resolved. In fact, I don't know of any marriage that doesn't have this type of complexity. For the most part, our differences are what creates marital tensions. Understanding and accepting the fact that your spouse is a person too and has the right to his or her own opinion and way of functioning will help minimize these tensions.

Alice and Charles

Alice told me that she grew up without heat or air conditioning. Her husband, Charles, liked their home to be summerlike during the winter and winter-like during the summer. Alice said that her body was unable to adjust to the outside temperatures when the indoor temperatures were so extreme. I suggested that instead of constantly arguing over the temperature in their home (one of the recurring challenges that interfered with the peace and harmony in their relationship), they should compromise with a maximum heat and a minimum cold setting.

In the winter, if Charles was still cold at the maximum heat setting (which they should settle on before the cold weather arrived), he could put on a warmer sweater or use a cozy blanket and Alice could wear a T-shirt. In the summer, they could leave the thermostat at the agreed-upon minimum cold setting so that the air turned on automatically when needed, and Charles could use a fan if he was still too warm.

I also suggested that Alice and Charles remind each other that this was a recurring problem and no fault of either of them. Allowing it to derail the harmony of their relationship would be unnecessarily damaging.

It's beneficial to a marriage for a couple to identify these recurring disagreements so that when they arise they will not be a constant source of irritation.

Remember not to make the challenge more
important than the marriage.

Double Standards

Some people are not aware of how their actions affect others.

Sonia and Eric

Sonia complained to me that she felt very unhappy in her relationship with Eric. She said that he lived by "double standards," that he was a very anal man who wanted everything in their home to be a certain way—showroom perfect (a negative tendency). He would reprimand her very harshly about something and then commit the same "crime" himself (another negative tendency). The example she gave was leaving a cabinet door ajar: he would lecture her sternly about how a cabinet door left open would eventually become misaligned, and yet he left the doors ajar himself.

Sonia felt he was being unfair and unreasonable, and she was becoming increasingly angry after each lecture, which occurred quite frequently. She felt that she practically could not move without his consent and that she was going to burst (a negative tendency) at his next "double standards" lecture. She loved Eric, but at the same time, she felt that his double standards were creating a rift between them.

I suggested that before she risked "bursting" and possibly ruining their relationship, she should think about the fact that Eric might not have been aware of his own behavior. When she had trouble believing that Eric could be so "blind," I explained to her that this scenario was actually quite common. Since he may not have been cognizant of the problem, I said, she needed to approach him with sensitivity.

I recommended that Sonia wait for the right time (after they had eaten dinner and had unwound from the day) and then gently say, "I would like to talk to you about something that's been bothering me—is now okay?" If he agreed, then she could continue: "I've noticed that you tell me not to do certain things, but then you do that same thing yourself. For example, you tell me not to leave the cabinet doors ajar, but you do it too, and often. To help you realize this, I will bring your attention to it when it happens—okay? The other thing I want to bring to your attention is the way you speak to me: you reprimand me very harshly. I'm your wife; I would appreciate being spoken to with kindness and respect. It would improve our relationship dramatically."

Eric agreed, although he doubted what Sonia was saying; he couldn't even imagine that he acted that way. He also had no idea that he spoke to her in such a manner, and he promised to be aware of his tone in the future.

Sonia was amazed at how unaware Eric was of his own behavior. I then explained to her that if something bothers us intensely about our spouse, most likely there is a similar characteristic within ourselves that we need to pay attention to. (See "Mirror, Mirror On Your Spouse," chapter 2.) Ironically, Sonia doubted that she displayed the same behavior (a negative tendency). I asked her to have an open mind and practice self-observation (see chapter 2).

Six months later, Sonia informed me, with some embarrassment, that she saw herself behaving much as Eric had, but under different circumstances. She would speak harshly to someone who questioned her opinion. In other words, she was "anal" about her opinion, and when someone questioned it, she felt she needed to "reprimand" him or her.

Sonia had been enlightened about herself through her challenge with Eric. They both grew from the experience. They now accept and understand each other and themselves better.

Fair Is Fair

It's important for couples to be fair in their marriage. If one spouse always wants his or her way, the other may start to feel resentful and unimportant. This will obviously create tension.

It's hard to believe, but for many couples, disagreements arise around vacations—a time when we want to relax and get away from stress. A vacation is not fun or rejuvenating if one spouse always wants to control what the destination is or what activities they partake in. To prevent arguments, it's a good idea for the couple to take turns choosing. For example, if she likes going to the beach in the morning and he likes going in the afternoon, they should compromise and cooperate, alternating between morning and afternoon, or finding a time that they can both be comfortable with.

During vacations, partaking in your spouse's interests and staying together as much as possible, even if the activity he or she has chosen doesn't appeal to you, is a wonderful way to invigorate the marriage. It might be fun—you never know!

Some couples prefer to vacation apart from each other, choosing to vacation with friends instead. This promotes separateness and may tear down the relationship in the long run.

In a marriage where a commitment has been made, there are two people involved; one can't always expect to have his or her way all the time.

Taking turns choosing activities and accompanying each other will revitalize a relationship. The same rule can be applied to other activities in all areas of life.

Loud but Not Clear

A special word about anger (otherwise known as an "adult temper tantrum"): raising your voice in an argument does not accomplish anything positive. It makes it impossible to resolve a disagreement amicably. It erodes the marital relationship and creates a negative cycle.

Never use anger against anyone unless he
or she is trying to cause you harm.

There are varying degrees of anger—from frustration, impatience, and annoyance to wrath and fury. Anger is very destructive to the angry person and, of course, to the person on the receiving end of it.

Anger can implode or explode. When anger implodes, it harms the angry person's physical body and emotional well-being. When it explodes, it can destroy relationships.

If you tune in to your body when you're angry and afterward, you will realize that many powerful chemicals are released into your system. These chemicals cause harm to your body. Initially you may feel a rush, but a few hours later, you may feel depressed and/or experience physical symptoms.

Adult temper tantrums are learned from childhood, and the root cause of them is the ego. When we learn humility, we experience growth. We must use our words appropriately instead of becoming emotional.

Many people deny having a temper. As children, they may have witnessed family members with anger issues and seen the destruction that anger could cause within a family. They do not wish to be associated with this kind of devastation, and so they will justify their angry behavior as passion, enthusiasm, frustration, annoyance, or any other term that makes it seem less damaging. It's of paramount importance to take responsibility for your actions and not justify them; this is critical to your marriage as well as your own growth.

It's crucial to realize that if you have a habit of becoming angry, this is what you are practicing and perfecting (practice makes perfect!). Whenever you feel a negative emotion, remember that it could be a learned bad habit. If you replace it with compassion, patience, acceptance, kindness, or understanding, you will not only feel much better about yourself, but you will also gain your spouse's respect.

It was even recorded in ancient times that Moses, one of the greatest and humblest prophets who ever lived, was denied entry into the Promised Land expressly because of his mistake of becoming angry.

Anger impairs your thinking and judgment.

As a result, you may be reckless with your life mate's feelings, creating deep hurt that will wear down your relationship.

What should you do when you feel yourself becoming angry with the one you love?

- Take some deep breaths—at least five or so. Inhale to the count of four, hold for the count of four, and exhale to the count of six.

- Before you respond, you can say in a kind way, "I will respond to you—just give me five minutes, please," and then work on defusing your emotions.
- Do whatever it takes to release that anger: beat or scream into a pillow, jump rope, or drink some calming tea.
- Remember to think before speaking to your loved one. It is worth the effort.

Hurting your spouse is like hurting yourself. Your loved one is your partner in life: if he or she is not happy, you will not be happy, and vice versa. Essentially, you are one.

The most effective way to defuse your life partner's negative emotions is by reacting not with anger or acquiescence, but with calmness. You can try offering calm responses like these:

- "Why are you talking to me like that? I'm your wife/ husband."
- "Let's talk when you have regained your self-control."
- "I'm on your side. Please refrain from speaking to me like that."
- "There's no need to speak to me with such anger. I'm your wife/husband, and I'm on your side."
- "Would you please use your words?"
- "Let's be constructive, not destructive."

Believe it or not, anger is a choice.

Even though your anger feels justified, you can choose to react with self-control, kindness, and compassion.

Anger is sometimes used to control or manipulate another person, but instead all it does is create mistrust. It's difficult for us to trust someone who raises his or her voice. If we open our hearts to such a person, we may feel vulnerable. We need to protect ourselves from his or her mishandled emotions; therefore, we may unintentionally withhold our love.

If you are the one with the temper, it's vital to learn how to express yourself in a composed way. You can take deep breaths or go into the next room to calm yourself. You can pause, think before you speak, and use your words appropriately. You can reframe the negative thinking that caused your anger in the first place, and control your emotions instead of letting them control you.

If you often overreact, your spouse may become reluctant to discuss his or her feelings with you. This may put your relationship in jeopardy.

If you wish to preserve your marriage and the love of your spouse, learning anger management would be highly beneficial. Controlling your anger is essential to your growth.

Taking your frustrations out on your spouse has consequences: it chips away at your relationship.

If your spouse is the one with anger issues, consider not allowing yourself to be the target. Try saying in a neutral way, "I can see that you are angry, and I want to talk to you, but not like this. Let's talk later." And then walk away. You can also try simple statements such as "You are shouting" or "You are raising your voice" or "You are yelling at me." This may make your spouse conscious of his or her behavior.

If your partner insists on talking while having an "adult temper tantrum," become a broken record and repeat what you just said (e.g., "Let's talk later.") until you are heard. Sometimes people can get so riled up that they can't hear what is being said to them. If repeating yourself makes your partner even more irate, then consider saying, "Think about whether you are overreacting."

Be conscious of the fact that anger has a strong ripple effect.

My friend's husband came home frustrated because his boss came to work in a bad mood. He took his frustration out on her, and in turn she wasn't patient with their children and then they got into trouble at school. Who knows who else was affected by one person's bad mood—their children's friends and their parents? The teacher and her family, and everyone *they* knew?

We have the power to direct which way the conflict will go by controlling our emotions; otherwise our emotions will control the argument. If the disagreement escalates, stop and say, "I need to take a five-minute break." Do some deep breathing or self-talk to regain composure. To defuse your spouse's negativity, it's more productive to stay centered and not react.

Emotions confuse the mind and will get in the way of resolving a challenge quickly and amicably. No one can make good decisions when he or she is emotional.

Raising your voice during a disagreement could be a learned behavior. We inherit many things from our parents, including how to resolve tension. If you witnessed your parents yelling at each other, then you may instinctively do the same thing—unless you consciously say to yourself that you will do things differently. You can unlearn this behavior and learn better ways to resolve issues, especially with the one you love.

Anger, no matter how we justify it, undermines the marital relationship. Anger is not passion or enthusiasm; it is destruction.

Fear is a common reason for anger; people become angry when something triggers their fear. Anger is also used as a form of manipulation or control. Many people have difficulties expressing themselves appropriately, and so they become frustrated and lash out.

If your spouse is angry and says, "I don't want to talk about it right now," or, "I want to be alone," do not insist on talking at that time. It is actually a good thing if your life partner does not want to discuss an issue when he or she is angry. Your partner may need some time to sort out his or her thoughts or just to cool off. You can then say, "Let's meet to discuss this in thirty minutes." Talking at a later time will prevent the disagreement from getting out of control.

Being kind and neutral is an alternative if you're not feeling loving. Being kind is not just a matter of being "nice"; it also means being respectful and caring about your life mate's feelings.

If a couple were to look back at their past arguments, they would clearly see that they could have had reasonable discussions without raising their voices and resolved their disagreements amicably. They would have learned and grown from the experience and fortified their relationship.

Dalia and Zack

Dalia admitted to me that when her husband, Zack, did not call to let her know that he was going to come home late, she would get angry and accuse him of being inconsiderate, and she would eventually escalate to yelling. They had spoken about this problem previously, yet he still didn't call her.

I suggested to Dalia that instead of becoming emotional, she could ask to speak to Zack (remembering to respect his time and space), and if he was okay with that, then she could say in a non-accusatory way, "I know that we have spoken about this before, but I really need you to call me if you are going to come home late. I care and worry about you. I also need to know what to do about dinner. It would be fair and considerate to me if you called to let me know. Can you give me confirmation that you agree to call me in the future when you are going to come home late?"

I urged Dalia to keep her conversation as short and direct as possible, considering that they had spoken about this issue before. Otherwise Zack would see it as dragging on too long and might become irate.

Obtaining some kind of agreement from Zack was important. If he still didn't call after Dalia spoke to him, she could say without sounding demanding, "You agreed to call me when you are going to be late. I need you to live up to your agreement. We should also talk about why this seems so difficult for you."

If Dalia was patient, I told her, she could help Zack correct an issue within himself. She would then have a deeper understanding of his dilemma while resolving the tension between them. This outcome would be measurably good for their relationship.

It's important to realize that it's your own emotionally charged thinking, not your spouse, that can make you angry. It is a choice: you can choose to let loose your emotions, or you can choose to be kind and express yourself in a constructive fashion. If you truly do not wish to become upset, no matter what your life partner says or does, your temper will not be aroused.

For example, instead of thinking, *That is so annoying—it is driving me nuts. I'm going to explode! I feel like I'm being pushed over the edge! He keeps doing that same thing over and over, even after we spoke about it!* consider reframing your thoughts this way: *He's doing that same thing again. I need to find another way of expressing myself to help him understand that it really bothers me. I must speak respectfully, because he is not doing this on purpose and I don't want to hurt his feelings.*

You need to refashion any unhealthy thoughts into ones that will improve you and your marriage.

Having a mental list of affirmations to help you defuse negative emotions is very important; after all, you do what your mind tells you. If you manipulate your thoughts to be more constructive, you will also have control over the disagreement.

Here are some examples of such affirmations:

- "I can control my emotions. I can be calm."
- "Breathe, relax. It's not the end of the world."
- "I am speaking to my love, so I don't want to hurt any feelings."
- "I want to work this out so that we can get back on track ASAP."
- "I want to resolve this challenge so that our marriage will be better for it."
- "I want to build our relationship and not wear it down."

Anger is the easy route to take; we want everyone to do things our way, in our time. While it is less convenient and takes more effort to pause, be patient, and think before you speak or act, if you were to do so, you might discover that you didn't have to become angry in the first place.

Jacob and Julie

Jacob explained that for three or four nights, he did not help Julie clean up the kitchen but instead went to relax and watch TV. They both worked, and he acknowledged that Julie was also tired by the end of the day.

Jacob said that Julie walked into the living room, where he was relaxing, and proceeded to verbally attack him. He told me that his natural instinct was to attack back. The exchange then escalated into a very loud and vicious disagreement.

He stated that Julie screamed, "You never help me!" which was not true. He said that he did help her, except for those three or four nights. And as it turned out, there was a reason for his failure to help her those few nights: he was distracted because he was having trouble with his supervisor at work. If Julie had approached him in a loving manner, she would have found out the reason and the argument could have been prevented.

I gave Julie an alternate scenario: she could walk over to him, sit down, give him a kiss on the cheek, and say, "I've noticed that you've stopped helping me clean up the kitchen. Why is that?" Then she could say, "Sorry you're having trouble with your supervisor. Let's talk about it while we clean up the kitchen together. I need your help; I'm tired too."

It's best not to become demonstrative in this kind of situation. This may lead you to lose self-control, which can be very damaging to the relationship.

*Most important, when you are angry, you
can't see your spouse's point of view.*

Just expressing yourself in a neutral tone can release your feelings of anger or hurt. Try saying, for example, "I felt very angry/hurt when you said what you said earlier."

If your spouse seems combative, you can say,

- "I don't want to fight with you. Let's discuss it in a better way."
- "Let's keep it constructive."
- "I can't discuss things with you when you are like this. Let's talk later."
- "This is not a big deal; let's not make it into one."
- "Let's not fight about this; it's not worth it."

When people are emotional, they may even say things they don't mean—a preventable problem. I love this line, which I heard in a movie: "Anger makes smart people do and say stupid things." The only appropriate use of anger is to create positive change or to protect yourself from harm.

Disagreeing

Some couples feel that because they disagree on many things, they are not compatible. There are a multitude of reasons couples might chronically disagree; simply being opposites will create this dilemma. For the most part, these couples are focusing on the negative rather than the positive aspects of their relationship.

When you focus on the positive aspects of your
spouse and marriage, your perspective will change.

An easy way to solve minor challenges that seem to have no resolution is to let them go. Trying to force your spouse to agree with your idea because you think it is best, when he or she feels equally right, will only create additional problems. If you feel you have a valid reason, you can ask your spouse to listen to your point of view. At the same time, you must have an open mind to hear your spouse's side.

If the disagreement is insignificant in the big picture, then it would be appropriate not to pursue a resolution. Making a big deal out of a transient situation that will not impact the future in any way just creates discord. Make the decision not to argue about things you can't agree on.

The Crank

If one or both spouses are in a bad mood, it is always best to delay discussing anything until the mood lifts.

Bad moods can be catchy. If one spouse is irritable, the other spouse can quickly become agitated as well, which may lead to a "spontaneous combustion" scenario.

It is a good idea for the cranky spouse to forewarn his or her partner, "I'm feeling a little off today. Please don't think that it has anything to do with you. I just need some time to shake it off."

Bad moods are usually not random. Sometimes they are caused by physical issues, such as pain, or psychological issues, such as emotional irritation. We must think about why we feel the way we do so that we can shake off bad moods as quickly as possible.

Louise Hay's extremely helpful book, *Heal Your Body: The Mental Causes for Physical Illness and the Metaphysical Way to Overcome Them*, will show you how your emotions can affect your physical body.

Avoidance

Avoiding confrontational discussions damages the marital relationship in the long term. If you "stuff" your frustrations and refrain from expressing yourself, you will eventually become resentful toward your spouse. An accumulation of many little irritations may eventually cause disharmony.

Resentments that are warehoused may cause you to suddenly explode with anger and destroy your relationship, or they may lead to a complete loss of emotions, resulting in a passionless marriage.

That said, not all issues need to be pointed out to your spouse. Some issues can be resolved within you. Ask yourself, *Am I being unnecessarily picky? Am I feeling out of sorts today? Maybe tomorrow I'll feel different.*

If an issue is so troublesome that it causes you to look at your spouse in a contrary way, you must either change your own negative perspective or speak to your spouse about it. If you avoid expressing your true feelings, your spouse may not understand your actions.

For example, if you feel taken for granted every night after cleaning up the kitchen alone while your spouse plays video games in the other room, he or she may think that you are simply cranky in the evenings and may not want to be around you. Your partner may not realize that you are in a bad mood because you are feeling resentful. If you express your true feelings in a gentle manner, explaining that you feel taken for granted and would appreciate help, your spouse will most likely cooperate. This will resolve the tension that regularly occurs after dinner.

Stonewalling

When a spouse says, "There's nothing more to talk about," or, "I don't want to talk about that," or, "What's there to talk about?" this is stonewalling. It cuts off communication between the partners. When there is no discussion, difficulties cannot be resolved.

The stonewaller may also try the silent treatment or shrug off any attempt that his or her partner makes to connect.

The spouse wishing to resolve the challenge could try again another time or say to the stonewaller in a neutral tone,

- "If you don't want to talk, then how do you suggest we resolve this issue?"

- "If you refuse to discuss this, you are cutting off communications. We won't be able to resolve this issue and we can't move forward, so let's make a time to talk."
- "I feel really upset about this. I need to talk to you about it so that I can put it behind me."

Stonewallers usually do not want to talk, so when they do agree to discuss a problem, conversation should be kept neutral and to the point.

Repetitive Action

If your spouse keeps repeating a behavior that you think is damaging or that you find very annoying, it would be highly beneficial to your marriage to bring it to his or her attention.

Shelley and Noah

Shelley said her husband, Noah, had a bad habit of showing up twenty to thirty minutes late for their weekly lunch dates. She rightly felt that her time was also valuable. Shelley explained that she was usually annoyed by the time Noah showed up, and that he always had some excuse—work, traffic, an important phone call. This seems to be a repetitive bad habit of Noah's (a negative tendency).

I asked Shelley to give Noah the benefit of the doubt and discuss the matter after their lunch. She could say, "Was everything okay at the office? You arrived twenty minutes late." If he gave her yet another excuse, she could then say, "I really enjoy and look forward to having lunch with you every week. I don't appreciate being kept waiting for twenty to thirty minutes. My time is also valuable. I feel like you are not placing any importance on our time together. I really enjoy our lunch dates and would like to continue. This happens often, and we have spoken about it before. What do *you* think we can do to resolve this issue?"

You must patiently help your spouse learn how to treat you. If you allow certain behaviors to continue, then your partner may think that this is the way he or she can behave. If you don't educate your spouse about how you would like to be treated, challenges will arise in the future.

If you have mentioned a specific situation to your spouse over and over again and your concern seems to be falling on closed ears, you must try a different way, using different words (their language) and a different manner, but always respectfully, to accomplish positive change.

Filter

It is vitally important to filter your speech, especially when you are emotional. Once you've said something, your spouse has heard it—it cannot be unheard.

Even if you say, "I'm sorry. I didn't mean what I said," your words went into your life mate's ears, mind, and heart. It may even change the way your spouse feels about you. Over the long term, a little unfiltered word here and there can add up and build resentments, damaging your relationship.

Our speech has a profound impact on other people. For example, the words a parent uses with his or her child can have a lifelong effect on that child's self-esteem and well-being.

The saying goes that "sticks and stones can break my bones, but words will never hurt me," but many people can testify that inappropriate words broke their hearts. So many people have been hurt and so many relationships have come to an end because of unfiltered words.

The words we use can create bridges or barriers. Words can build or destroy relationships. Words can create a great love or break a precious heart, can create trust or mistrust. Words have created world wars, and words can create world peace.

Think before you speak. If you don't have anything good to say in the moment, take a few deep breaths and remember that you are speaking to the most important person in your world, your life mate.

Children

Each spouse has his or her own ideas regarding child rearing and wants to apply those concepts to raising his or her own children. Tension develops when a married couple's opinions about parenting are contradictory.

For example, if he was raised with strictness and she was raised with leniency, they will obviously disagree on how to correct their children's behavior. If they wish to preserve peace and harmony in their home, they can work out a compromise and find balance in their disciplining techniques. Their children will then be raised somewhere in between, with neither strictness nor leniency.

It is more practical for parents to discuss how to deal with a discipline challenge before confronting the child. Parents should be united so that the child can see that he or she cannot play one parent against the other. It's not beneficial for children to witness their parents arguing about how to deal with a discipline problem. It's best for such discussions to take place behind closed doors.

Raising children can lead to marital tensions, but if the parents collaborate for their children's benefit, ultimately they can create a well-balanced home environment.

A wise person once told me that a parent must earn his or her child's respect. A child cannot love a parent he or she doesn't respect.

Children are extremely affected by what their parents do and say and are watching and learning the bad as well as the good. Parents are their children's role models, and how they behave will affect their children's future. Behaviors, mannerisms, and even words get passed down from one generation to the next.

When parents show their children that they are partners in life first and foremost, they instill within them a secure sense of the family unit. As a parent, you can demonstrate this by doing things such as

- greeting your life mate first, before the children or the dog;
- buying your spouse's favorite treat and making sure everyone knows that "this is only for Daddy/Mommy";
- sitting with your spouse whenever possible, and not always having the kids between you.

Taking actions that create a strong marital foundation will result in children who feel secure in their own lives and their future.

Finances

Many couples say that financial issues are the number one challenge in their marriage.

The best way to solve this kind of dilemma is to work together. Attacking the problem is far more constructive than attacking each other. A dispute over finances can be overcome quite quickly if the partners sit down, collaborate, and draw up a plan of action.

Arguing about money just makes a bad situation worse. Two people can overcome a financial issue better than one person on his or her own.

Many couples have the challenge of one spouse being frugal and the other being a big spender. If that's the case with your marriage, make the time to discuss this challenge; don't let it remain a sore point. The frugal partner can say in a kind way, "Your frequent spending on things we don't necessarily need makes me feel very anxious and insecure regarding our finances. I don't feel respected or valued as your partner. You know how I feel about having savings. Let's figure out how we can reorganize our financial situation so that we can both be comfortable."

A financial expert, bank, or credit union may be able to offer advice on how to resolve financial issues. Often just opening up a separate, limited account for the big spender will suffice.

If problems regarding finances or children can't be resolved, it's always good to seek an opinion from outside the circle of friends and family, such as a rabbi, priest, mediator, or financial advisor. Advice from family and friends is usually biased and may not be advantageous to the couple.

Preferences

If it's allowed to, a difference in opinions or preferences regarding artwork, furniture, styles, colors, and other aesthetic matters can create disharmony. Some couples may feel they are so different from each other in this regard that they are incompatible. In a case like this, it's beneficial for the couple to focus on their commonalities and appreciate and accept each other's differences. This change in mindset can be accomplished by finding things they enjoy together, or by mutually agreeing that the issue is more important to one spouse than the other.

Rob and Libby

Rob explained that he felt strongly about having colored marbles in the vase that was the centerpiece of their dining room table. Libby wanted fresh flowers in the vase periodically. Rob felt that fresh flowers were a waste of money and they didn't have money to waste.

I pointed out to Rob and Libby that the marbles-versus-flowers argument was a very insignificant part of their "big picture." Whoever had the stronger feelings about what should go in the vase should make the decision.

Libby's preference was not as important to her as Rob's was to him, so they settled on colored marbles. Libby was happy with the suggestion to plant more flowers in their garden.

If one spouse always insists on his or her own preferences or opinions, then the other could say informatively, "We are in a partnership; I am the other half of that partnership. I am a person too, and my opinions and preferences are also valid. They may not be the same as yours, but that doesn't make them wrong—just different from yours. To be fair, I would like my preferences and opinions to be considered also."

It is really not worth the stress or the wear and tear on a marriage to argue about the little things. If couples would realize that their relationship is more important than having their way, they would experience more harmony.

Make it your preference to have peace and harmony in your marriage.

Benefit of the Doubt

It's very important to your relationship to give your spouse the benefit of the doubt when a disagreement occurs. You could have heard him or her incorrectly, or you could have misunderstood. We like to think that such problems are our spouse's fault, but we can't always put the blame there.

Michelle and Justin

Justin told me that he had a toothache one morning, so he already was in a bad mood when his wife, Michelle, began suggesting natural remedies to help him. Justin explained that he knew those remedies would not take the discomfort away immediately; all he was interested in was an instant pain reliever. When Michelle left the room, he thought she was insulted because he wasn't listening to her suggestions. He also felt that she wasn't being patient. This pushed him over the edge, and an argument ensued.

Michelle told me that she knew Justin could focus on only one thing at the time, and that was his pain. So she left the room to make breakfast, thinking that when he was ready to talk, he would ask her about the natural remedies, which she knew would help alleviate the pain.

I asked Michelle to think about her part in the scene. She realized that before exiting the room, instead of leaving him to guess, she could have mentioned that it was getting late and she needed to leave for work, adding that he could ask her about the natural remedies when he was ready. She also realized that because Justin was very uncomfortable, she should have chosen not to argue with him.

I asked Justin to think about his part in the scene. He realized that he'd jumped to a conclusion and should have given Michelle the benefit of the doubt.

Some people complain that their spouse seems to be the most thoughtless person in the world: he does things only for himself; she thinks only about her own needs; he forgets to do things that were asked of him; she appears to be totally self-absorbed. But those spouses must be given the benefit of the doubt.

If we delved into their backgrounds and their psyches, perhaps we would find that something in their childhood caused them to live in their own protective world, oblivious to anyone else. It's also possible that they simply do not realize that they need to make room for their spouse in their lives. There could be a multitude of reasons for this behavior.

Expecting your partner's behavior to automatically change can prove disappointing. He or she may not know a different way of behaving and may never have had a reason to learn any other way. You must not be impatient with your partner for appearing to be thoughtless, because most likely you were subconsciously aware of this characteristic from the start. You must patiently help your life mate learn a better way of functioning, which will in turn help with your own growth.

Your spouse may be very willing to learn another way. Instead of being hurt or offended by his or her "thoughtlessness," teach your life partner in a gentle and kind manner to be more mindful of your presence in his or her life. For example, if your spouse brings a fork to the table and does not bring one for you also, instead of becoming upset, you could say, "Please, would you be more mindful of me next time and bring a fork for me as well? There are two of us in this relationship." Your spouse may need some reminding for a while until he or she has learned the new way.

It's to your own advantage to give the benefit of the doubt to your spouse if he or she happens to do something annoying. Presuming he or she knew beforehand that it would be upsetting but did it anyway will lead to an argument. Assuming that it was done on purpose, in order to annoy you, will also lead to a negative reaction. Concluding that your life mate did not realize how his or her actions would affect you will produce a more positive outcome.

If your spouse is unaware of the negative effects of his or her actions, you can patiently say, "Please don't do that—it really makes me feel uncomfortable." If your partner simply forgot, you can remind him or her: "Please don't do that—it really turns me off. We have spoken about this before, so please try not to do that again, okay?" or try his or her language (see Chapter 4 – "Say What?")

Memories

When discussing a challenge with your spouse, it's best not to bring up past issues—that may cause additional discord and most likely will escalate the argument.

Our memories are not always as accurate as we would like to believe. They can be contaminated by the passage of time, by our perceptions, by our emotions, and by anything in the environment at the moment the memory was created.

Alison was absolutely certain that her best friend, Karen, said something disparaging about her when Alison announced her fourth pregnancy to a gathering of friends and family. Karen confirmed that she would never say anything denigrating to or about her best friend. The only explanation Karen could think of was that at the time of the announcement, someone else made a negative comment while Alison was looking at Karen, which caused Alison to have a contaminated memory of the event. Yet Alison was so convinced that her memory was correct that she no longer wanted to be friends with Karen. How sad!

You can never be certain of the accuracy of your memories. Using them as evidence against your life partner without proof could cause unnecessary damage to your marriage.

A Wise Action

One of the wisest actions a couple can take is to avoid having an emotional disagreement, which often leads to a communication breakdown.

Psychologists say that it is good to argue. But it is important to understand that they are advocating not quarreling, but discussing or debating. Quarreling is destructive and wears down the relationship.

A quarrel can easily get out of control. It must be stopped before someone gets hurt. It's an easy path to take, but resist the temptation. It is much harder to control your emotions so that a constructive conversation can take place.

If you're tempted to quarrel, ask yourself, *Do I really want to do this? Is it worth the stress?* or *Am I in control, or am I just running with my anger or frustrations?*

If a disagreement develops into a quarrel, one spouse can say, "Let's stop—we are getting off track. Let's start over," or simply take a five-minute break to do some deep breathing.

Chose defusing tones and words such as these:

- "We can do this constructively."
- "We can do better."
- "I know we can work this out."

Avoid escalating tones and words such as these:

- "You did that on purpose, didn't you?"
- "It's all your fault."
- You're just saying that to annoy me."

An emotional disagreement can very quickly turn into an argument about what and how things were said, and even past issues can get involved. In the process, the original cause of the disagreement can be forgotten. The couple will then feel exhausted, having accomplished nothing constructive.

If the dispute is handled purposefully—that is, if both spouses keep in mind that they are talking to their chosen one—they will tend to be more kind and patient. They will also listen more, try harder to see their partner's point of view, and be more flexible in their positions. They will be willing to resolve the tension amicably in order to preserve their marriage.

This is a test of your growth: the more self-control you apply and the more constructively you handle challenges, the more you are growing.

Be the One

If a discussion with your spouse is becoming destructive in some way, be the one to stop arguing. Allowing a dispute to get out of control just generates negativity in your marriage. You can say something like this:

- "Let's stop. This is getting out of hand—we need to take a break."
- "This is not constructive. Let's talk later, when we are both calm."
- "There's no need to get so upset. I'm on your side."

You can also use a hand gesture, such as a time-out signal, that you and your spouse previously agreed upon, followed by an agreement to talk later, after a reasonable amount of cooling-off time.

Don't wait for your spouse to stop the argument—be "the one." Also, be the one to initiate reconciliation when the time feels right, and be the one to bring the relationship back to normal as soon as possible.

If you are the one who is more emotionally mature, finding a way to help your spouse become more emotionally mature as well, without preaching or lecturing, will strengthen the bond in your relationship.

You can gently say to your spouse, "I always seem to be the one who monitors our discussions. You need to take responsibility for your words and actions. Maybe then our disagreements will be more constructive, okay?"

You Don't Look Marvelous to Me

When you feel angry on the inside, it's natural that your outside will not be as attractive as when you are feeling loving and happy. During an argument, you may not see your partner as being as appealing as he or she was before. This means that you have allowed yourself to view him or her in a very negative way. Unfortunately, this makes it easier to be unkind with your thoughts, speech, and actions. It's imperative to work very hard on focusing on resolving the argument and not on how your partner looks when he or she is upset.

Once the disagreement has been resolved and apologies accepted, and forgiveness has been given, you will again be physically attracted to each other.

If the problem has been improperly handled and allowed to continue for some time, this may create a scenario where someone outside the marriage seems appealing. You must not allow yourself to be tempted by another person's appearance or be flattered by his or her attention. This will place a barrier between you and your spouse, which will prevent the relationship from healing.

This is another test of your growth: how you
conduct yourself during a rough patch.

As I previously mentioned, challenges are opportunities to strengthen your marriage and attain a higher understanding of yourself and your spouse.

Same Side

A key to successful marriage is for couples to remember that they are a team—they're on the same side.

Many couples view each other as adversaries when there is a disagreement, making them opponents rather than partners. Some people even create alliances with their friends or family members against their life mates.

Too many ideas and too much well-meaning advice from friends and family can create confusion for the couple and may cause further discord. If it is necessary to seek help from a third party, it's more productive to go to someone they respect and trust from outside their circle, or even a professional, such as a mediator.

When you feel that your spouse is being challenging (nagging, complaining, arguing), before you react, think about what message he or she is trying to convey. Remember that your spouse is on your side. Ask yourself, *What is my spouse trying to bring to my attention?* If your thoughts are negative, such as *What a complainer/grouch/nag,* tensions will arise and nothing will be accomplished.

It's possible that your spouse may not be able to verbalize his or her thoughts at that moment. Asking or guessing what he or she is attempting to express ("What's making you so unhappy? Is it...?") can help direct the conversation.

If your spouse is feeling frustrated for reasons that have nothing to do with you, but he or she is taking it out on you, you could say in a neutral manner, "You probably don't realize this, but you seem off or frustrated lately. I feel like you have been very snappy and impatient with me. It makes me feel anxious when you take your frustrations out on me. I'm on your side, so please don't do that. Would you like to talk about whatever is bothering you?"

When both partners keep in mind that they are on the same side, they can work together and solve any challenge that presents itself.

Humor to the Rescue

Some couples bring humor into their disagreements to alleviate any negative emotions.

My friend told me that her husband was upset with her for letting their beautiful potted plants dry out. An argument ensued, but then her husband said, "Don't speak like that in front of the plants." She started laughing, he laughed too, and the conflict was soon forgotten.

Never Quit

A couple must never quit trying to resolve the challenges that arise in their marriage. They should continuously experiment with different words and ways until each can understand what the other is attempting to communicate.

Brittany and Rich

Brittany complained to me that she was at her wit's end with Rich's obvious and prolific "looking" at other women (a negative tendency). She stated that it was very embarrassing, especially when they were with friends. She had mentioned it to Rich from time to time through the years, but he always became annoyed, telling her not to be so insecure.

I suggested that Brittany experiment with a different way of saying what she usually said (a negative tendency), which obviously wasn't working. I asked her to try the following: "Rich, I am not questioning your fidelity. I know what a loyal and faithful husband you are. When you look at other women like that, it makes me feel like I'm not enough for you and you are always looking for better. I also feel very disrespected. You are right: it does make me feel insecure, because I don't really know where I stand with you. It harms our relationship."

Rich had felt that Brittany was always questioning his fidelity. He now understood why she was upset by his "looking." He hadn't realized that it was harmful to their relationship, and he began working hard to eliminate the bad habit.

By using a different strategy to resolve their challenge, Brittany helped Rich and herself refine their negative tendencies and transform their marriage.

Obstacles

The following things can create obstacles when a couple is attempting to resolve a disagreement:

- **Negative facial expressions** such as rolling or squinting the eyes, curling the lip, shaking the head, and so forth, can undermine constructive communication.
- **Name calling** will add to the argument and create resentment in the long term. Even if you disparage your spouse mentally, you can cause yourself to lose respect for your spouse and view him or her in a negative way. You may think that your private thoughts can't be heard, but your partner will know, because thoughts are reflected in attitudes and behavior.
- **Put-downs, shaming, or negative comments** make your partner feel bad, and that means your discussions with him or her will not be constructive. For example, avoid comments like "You don't know what you are talking about," "That's just silly," or "You're acting like a child."
- **Labeling** through comments like "You are so overly sensitive/stubborn" creates more discord.

- **Bullying** is extremely destructive and always has negative consequences for a marriage. Some people bully their spouses in order to get their way, even if they are in the wrong. If your partner does this to you, ask him or her, "Are you trying to bully me?"
- **Manipulation** creates mistrust in a relationship.
- **Lies** destroy the foundation of a marriage.
- **Profanity** creates a negative cycle in a relationship. It is disempowering to the one who uses the bad language, as well as to the person on the receiving end.
- **Blaming** is the easiest thing to do. Blaming your spouse relieves you of your responsibility from your part in the disagreement. Ask yourself, *What is my part in this?*
- **Telling your spouse what to say or do** with comments like "You can't speak to me that way" or "Stop yelling at me" isn't constructive. Try to be more diplomatic: "I would appreciate you not speaking to me so disrespectfully."
- **Interrupting** is counterproductive. We don't feel heard when another person constantly interrupts. Try saying in a neutral way, "I would like to finish what I'm saying, please." Then keep it short so that your spouse can have a turn to speak.
- **Not listening** leads to miscommunication. If you are busy thinking about how you are going to respond, you may not hear your partner correctly and he or she will not feel heard.
- **Past issues** should stay in the past. It is always best to keep to the present discussion. Past issues just add to the argument.
- **Not being open to compromise** is unrealistic. Why wouldn't you want to be open to compromise with the one you love? You can't have everything your way all the time. Be willing; be cooperative.
- **Resentments** arise when you haven't been communicating your concerns, don't express yourself appropriately, or don't make it comfortable for your spouse to express his or her concerns. When you feel resentful, you might

be tempted to use words like *You always* or *You never*, which is usually not the case. Expressing your concerns, no matter how small you think they are, will prevent a buildup of resentments.

- **Negative childhood experiences** can affect the way you communicate. You may have inappropriate, automatic reactions to your "buttons" being pushed, such as bursting out with anger before knowing the whole story. It's important to be aware of these tendencies and understand why you feel the way you do. Sometimes your spouse will unknowingly push your buttons, which can help you become aware of them. If you are already conscious of your buttons, let your partner know what they are.
- **Hot weather** can cause us to be less patient and more argumentative.
- **A bad diet** can cause us to feel irritable. Food affects our mood and our relationships.
- **Hormonal imbalances** such as PMS, midlife changes, menopause, and thyroid imbalances can be reasons for challenges in a relationship. It's imperative to recognize you feel out of balance and not blame your spouse for your discomfort. (For more on hormones, see chapter 7.)
- **Physical ailments**, often accompanied by constant pain, and pharmaceutical medication, can cause a person to become irritable and impatient. Helping your spouse with his or her pain management, such as by offering a massage or doing research on natural remedies and therapies, will be beneficial to you both.
- **Impatience** is damaging to a marital relationship. Be willing to listen to your spouse's point of view, and be willing to spend some time trying to resolve the tension.
- **Not having an open mind**—whether that means refusing to cooperate with your spouse, refusing to listen to your spouse's point of view, or refusing to consider the fact that you may be partly responsible for the conflict—creates more dissension in the relationship. You may have

started the argument without realizing it, or you may not have started it but responded in a way that continued it.

- **Mind reading** can cause miscommunication. You might think you know what your spouse's thoughts are, but it is also a possibility that you could be completely wrong. Don't assume; ask.
- **Threats** will diminish trust, and the relationship will deteriorate in the long run.

Reconnecting

After an argument, especially one that lasts for more than a few hours, the couple may feel a little uncomfortable around each other. If the challenge has been resolved, they should work at putting it behind them so they can start rebuilding their relationship as soon as possible.

A good way to reconnect is to do something fun together that involves interacting in a positive way, such as

- going for a walk;
- going to the beach;
- having a picnic in a park;
- playing a fun game;
- making popcorn and watching an uplifting movie.

Helpful Steps to Take

The following actions are helpful for resolving conflicts:

- **Try to see your spouse's point of view.** This is very important. By doing this, you will be able to understand your spouse's reaction and thinking, even though you may not agree with them. Very often an argument can even be avoided this way.

- **Apologize.** If you know that you made a mistake, offering a sincere apology can end the disagreement before things get out of hand. It can also reestablish a connection after you've cooled off from an argument ("Sorry we had a problem earlier.") This does not necessarily mean admitting that you were in the wrong; it simply means acknowledging that there was friction and you could have done better.
- **Forgive.** This is for your sake as well as your relationship's. When you don't forgive, you become hard-hearted, which will create even more discord in your marriage. When you remember that your spouse is your "forever" partner, forgiving becomes easier. When you keep in mind that your spouse would not intentionally do something that would upset you, it is even easier. Remind yourself that you are not perfect either, that you too have made mistakes and unintentionally upset your life mate at some point. Forgiveness is a must.
- **Make a commitment.** Promising to try to avoid the same mistake in the future gives your spouse confidence and trust in your love.
- **Cooperate.** If you want your spouse to be cooperative, you must be cooperative also.

The following is a summary of how to manage a disagreement:

- Before responding, take some deep breaths and calm any negative emotions. Know that you are responsible for your own emotions and that you can choose to be constructive instead of being out of control and angry.
- Have affirmations ready to help you maintain balanced emotions.
- Ask yourself what your part is.
- How you react to and handle the argument will determine its outcome.
- The goal is to resolve your disagreement in a dignified manner so that the relationship will be strengthened.

- Resist the temptation to blame.
- Remind yourself that you are talking to the one you love and will be spending the rest of your life with.
- Remember that the two of you are on the same side.
- Even when you don't feel loving, you can still be kind and respectful.
- Think before you speak.
- Try very hard to see your spouse's point of view.
- Start sentences with "I feel" and not with "You."
- Speak in a neutral tone, without an attitude and without being accusatory.
- Be willing to cooperate and compromise.
- Remember that apologizing can initiate healing.
- Forgive easily—this is your life.
- Reconciling after a short cooling-off period helps the relationship get back on track.
- To handle a challenge successfully, please be sure to review chapters 1 through 4.

Part of creating a strong marital foundation and future is going through the "thick and thin" together. You must realize that ups and downs are a part of life and don't mean that your relationship is not working. What will put your marriage in jeopardy is focusing too much on the difficulties and not enough on the good times.

Ultimately, it is always best to communicate so that problems do not develop into resentments. *How* you communicate is the key.

If you seek peace in your relationship, you *will* create harmony in your marriage. If you start with peace in your home, it will spread to everything that you do, to everyone in your environment, and from there to the rest of the world.

Key Points

- Marriage is a partnership. Both spouses are accountable for what happens in their relationship.
- All challenges have a very important purpose. When we overcome them in a constructive way, we grow. When we grow, we become happier, more secure, and more successful in this world.
- Tension happens at some point in all relationships.
- Your spouse is not an opponent that you need to overcome and conquer.
- The disagreement is not more important than the marriage.
- If you don't feel loving during an argument, you can still be kind and respectful.
- If you focus on the positive aspects of your relationship, your negative perceptions will change.
- You must patiently help your spouse learn how to behave toward you.
- You must be the one to stop the communication breakdown.
- During a rough patch, your spouse may not look as attractive to you as he or she did before. You must therefore not be tempted by the appearance or flattery of other people.
- Never stop trying different ways to create peace and harmony in your relationship.

Chapter 6

Rekindling the Passion

They're faithfully working on transitioning their relationship into a river of deepening love and unrelenting strength while preserving that sweet, gentle warmth that enveloped them when they first realized their love for each other. He searches her beautiful brown eyes for that glowing spark he once saw, hoping against hope that it is still there. Instead, he joyfully finds a roaring fire of love that's been held in abeyance, longing for his attention. His heart pounds with excitement.

♥

A key to successful marriage is realizing that rekindling the passion is not as difficult as you may think. The love that was initially ignited and then sealed with a Sacred Vow is always there.

Think of a fire that has burned down, with only the logs left to glow. If more logs are added and the ones that are still glowing are carefully stoked, the fire will once again rekindle.

When the union between a husband and wife is sacred, the passion that exists between their opposite energies fuels the building of the relationship. If the union is not sacred, then the passion becomes consuming and destructive. A marriage, like a house, needs a good foundation to stand securely.

Cultivating sanctity in the relationship fortifies and strengthens the marital foundation.

You can cultivate sanctity by being gentle, kind, respectful, loyal, and faithful; by valuing each other's roles; by being careful not to offend; by taking an interest in and thinking positively about each other; by doing things together and doing things for each other; by being important to each other; and, of course, by loving through the downs as well as the ups.

If a couple has allowed their passion to diminish, they will say things like "We have grown apart," "We just don't love each other anymore," "We don't have anything in common anymore," "We don't get along anymore," "We don't talk anymore," or "I feel lonely in our relationship."

Usually passion declines because a couple's primary attention has been placed not on their marriage, but elsewhere. Rekindling the passion must begin with you. Ask yourself, *What was my part in the problem, and how can I improve my marriage?*

Rebuilding

Couples must change certain ways and habits they have fallen into that may have caused the decline, and then the direction of the marriage will be a more positive one.

An immediate action they can take is to stop doing things that damages their relationship and start doing things that strengthens it. If there is constant discord, the arguing, bickering, and blaming must stop. One partner can say, "What are we doing? Let's stop this—we are ruining our relationship! Let's make time to talk about what's going on."

After a short cooling-off period, the rebuilding process can begin. The discussion can commence with "I love you, and I don't want all this negativity between us. I want us to be happy and harmonious, as I know we can be and have been in the past. Can you please help me figure out what's going on and how we can get our relationship back on track?"

If there is no communication and the partners are feeling emotionally flat toward each other, then they must make the time and effort to open up a line of communication in a nonhostile way.

When you and your spouse are upset with each other, your actions are distancing and separating. You must change this situation as soon as possible. Start with small steps such as these:

- Make a cup of tea or coffee for your spouse—the way he or she likes it.
- Do things for him or her without being asked.
- The first thing to go in a relationship is politeness. Start reincorporating the words *please* and *thank you* and other polite gestures into your communication.
- Be more respectful and considerate toward your spouse.
- Give him or her space and privacy if it is needed.
- Be willing to cooperate.
- Flash a genuine smile.

Change your thoughts about your life mate from negative to more positive.

If you are constantly thinking, *I am so unhappy in my marriage, My spouse is not the right one for me,* or, *This is not working,* then it will be impossible to rekindle the passion between you, and your relationship will continue to decline. Constant negative thinking can ruin a marriage. Checking your negative thoughts and not aligning yourself with them will immediately change your perspective.

Stalemate

Sometimes a couple will reach a point where both parties are uncooperative and unwilling to compromise. Each has his or her "list" of changes the other partner must make in order for the relationship to move forward. This situation can create a rift and may even cause the couple to separate. The obstacle could be pride or stubbornness, or one spouse may simply feel that he or she is in the right.

Don't wait for or expect your spouse to make the first move. Be the one to say, "Okay, we seem to be in a stalemate. Let's sit down and try to work things out like two reasonable adults." This is not a sign of giving in, but an act of moving the relationship forward.

You must be willing to negotiate and compromise. Your thought process could be something like this: *I want this to work, so I must be willing to compromise and cooperate. I won't be giving anything up because compromising will benefit me and our marriage in the long run. This is my life partner.*

Agreeing to even one thing is a step toward ending the stalemate and moving forward.

The Balancing Act

*A key to successful marriage is creating
balance between learning and growing and
having fun together. Otherwise, the passion
between the couple will be consuming.*

By the time they reach adulthood, most people are somewhat negatively inclined. It takes effort and consistent practice to live with a more positive outlook.

At the beginning of a relationship, couples are very focused on each other's positive qualities and their commonalities. But once the courtship and honeymoon are over, they may begin to notice and focus on each other's shortcomings, which were always there but were ignored. Over time, they may allow their views of each other to subtly change from positive to negative, and that negative view is what many couples keep building on. They do not maintain the sweet, warm gentleness they had when they were courting.

*A key to successful marriage is realizing
that having a negative view of your spouse
distorts every aspect of your relationship.*

You may start to develop negative patterns of thinking regarding your spouse. This will cause you to become overcritical of your partner and focus more on his or her flaws, bringing them out even more.

When someone has a contrary pattern of thinking, those initial good thoughts about his or her spouse may become distorted. For example, earlier in the relationship, he may have thought, *I like how calm and relaxed she is,* and then a few years later, he may think, *She is so lazy—always putting things off!* Initially she may have thought, *I love how tidy and organized he is,* only to think later, *He's so anal! Everything has to be just so. Can't he just relax and not be so uptight all the time?*

> *A key to successful marriage is maintaining a positive view of your spouse. This is one of the most important values in a lasting relationship.*

When you *always* work on focusing on your spouse's positive qualities—just as couples do when they are courting—these good attributes become magnified and the imperfections fade. Then one day you will say to yourself, *I can't believe I had those unflattering thoughts about my spouse. I see her so differently now!*

> *Your marriage is a reflection of your thoughts and actions toward your spouse. If your demeanor is negative, your marriage will be contentious. Conversely, if your thoughts and actions are positive, your marriage will be more harmonious.*

Comparing

Comparing your spouse to any other person creates feelings within you that are incongruent with a happy marriage. Successful and happy couples don't compare their partners to anyone.

We all have positive and negative qualities. Some people see another person with an attribute they admire and say to themselves, *I wish my spouse were more like that.* If that's your habit, remember that you are seeing only one small part of that person, who may not be what your fantasies have led you to believe. He or she could be the most difficult person in the world to live with. You can't really get to know and experience someone until you live with that person.

Comparing your spouse to any person in Hollywood is extremely unrealistic. Everyone who appears on stage or on screen, big or small, has undergone hours of makeup and preparation. These people have been transformed and do not look the way they do when they wake up in the morning.

I know of a man whose wife cooked and took very good care of him for twenty-seven years. Nevertheless, his fantasies got the better of him, and he left her for a woman fifteen years younger, saying that his ex-wife did not compare. However, this younger woman did not cook for him, and she spent his money irresponsibly. She did not care how hard he worked; she was not frugal like his ex-wife. When he lost his money due to a bad investment, she left him. He ended up alone, with many regrets. His ex-wife would have stood by him. She had helped him become successful and most likely would have helped him regain his success. His second wife was much younger and more ambitious. They did not have the many years and experiences together that build a strong marital foundation.

The lesson: the grass is not greener on the other side.

Another comparison that must not be made is between the romantic relationships in movies, on TV, or in romance novels and from our own experience. Romantic relationships on the screen and in books are exaggerated. These scenes are meant to stir the emotions of the person who is watching or reading them. In reality, most people do not experience constant fireworks in their romance. Usually after the initial attraction, love takes time to mature and grow in a steady manner, and it feels stronger sometimes than at other times. Only in Hollywood can there be a romantic relationship of fairy-tale proportions.

If you compare your romantic relationship to movie romances or the romantic imagination of an author, you may begin to feel disappointed. All humans are imperfect; therefore, it's natural that human relationships will not be harmonious 100 percent of the time. Life and marriages sometimes go through rough patches, and this is normal.

It's also not practical to compare your marriage to anyone else's. We all know "that couple" who seemed to have the perfect relationship until they got divorced. You never know what goes on behind other people's closed doors.

Every relationship is in a different phase of the marital journey. However, if you see a quality in someone else's marriage that you admire, then strive to incorporate it into yours. You can say to your spouse, "Look how sweetly that couple communicates with each other. Isn't that wonderful? I would love for us to be like that. Do you think we can work on being that way?"

The same process can be employed regarding a harmful quality that you witness in someone else's relationship: "The way that couple communicates seems very damaging to their marriage. Let's be sure not to do that."

R-E-S-P-E-C-T

A key to successful marriage is always
maintaining respect for your life mate.

You can't love someone you don't respect. You must respect your spouse as an individual and as a person with needs, desires, and dreams that may be contrary to your own, as a person who needs his or her own space and whose time is also valuable.

It's almost impossible to become angry with someone you respect. In fact, displaying anger toward your spouse is a lack of respect.

You can't behave toward your spouse any way you want to. Your spouse is a person, and the most important person in your life. You must speak to and treat your spouse according to his or her sensibilities so that harmony can be achieved.

*When you feel respected by your spouse,
you feel valued as a partner.*

What are some of the ways you can maintain respect for your spouse?

- Realize that your spouse wants to share his or her life with you.
- Be grateful for what he or she brings to the relationship.
- Make sure not to lower his or her esteem in your eyes with negative thinking.
- Don't take him or her for granted.
- Focus on his or her good attributes rather than shortcomings.
- Acknowledge that you are imperfect; therefore don't expect him or her to be perfect.
- Check your thinking and make sure you hold him or her in a positive light.
- Be active in trying to fill his or her needs.

Acceptance

*A key to successful marriage is for couples to
accept each other's needs and ways, even if
they are different or contrary. This is of primary
importance in creating marital harmony.*

When you feel accepted as you are, you feel loved and valued. Whether or not you realize it, your spouse's unique ways were part of his or her initial attraction. These differences are your teachers; they help you grow. They teach you how to refine yourself—to be patient, accepting, tolerant of ways you may not agree with. They teach you to love selflessly, to love the whole person regardless of what you might perceive as his or her faults.

To someone else, your partner's imperfections may not be irritating at all. For example, a woman may think that her husband is opinionated, while another person might think his opinions are intelligent and must be heard.

You have flaws too, and you expect your spouse to accept them along with your good attributes.

Boundaries

Setting boundaries in a relationship maintains respect between partners. Without boundaries, the marriage may get out of balance. They must be persistently and consistently gently enforced or partners may become confused. Boundaries let each partner know how the other would like to be treated.

When spouses overstep each other's boundaries, there is tension in the marriage. Each partner may have different ways of doing things yet achieve good results. Trying to force your life partner to do things your way will create dissension. By being controlling, you are implying that your way is better and you know what's best. We all have our own way of doing things, and that's what makes this world such an interesting place. Setting boundaries strengthens the marital relationship.

Harry and Gail

Gail told me that Harry loathed doing repairs and odd jobs around the house and needed her assistance. She lamented that he would then become annoyed and frustrated and take out his feelings on her. My suggestion to Gail was that she gently lay down a boundary and say to Harry in a firm but kind way, "If you take your frustrations out on me, I will not help you," and that each time he needed her assistance, she could remind him, "I'll only help you if you don't take your frustrations out on me." I encouraged Gail to be consistent and persistent in enforcing her boundaries.

When Gail updated me, she said that Harry very quickly learned not to take his frustrations out on her—if he wanted her help. It was just a matter of changing a bad habit. To reinforce her boundaries in a positive way, I recommended that Gail mention to Harry how pleasant it was doing repair work with him around their home.

When your spouse endeavors to alter his or her ways for your sake, you must not take it for granted. Your life mate cares about you. He or she made those changes because you asked, and would not have done so if it weren't for your request. Showing appreciation for the effort—and it is an effort—will help the next time you ask for another change.

Cooperation

You must be willing to cooperate with your spouse, even if you are out of your comfort zone. Cooperation builds trust and togetherness; it is critical for strengthening the foundation of your relationship. After all, think about the person you are cooperating with: your life mate!

Gillian and Barry

Gillian explained that she was in the middle of making dinner when there was a neighborhood blackout. She asked Barry to call the utility company so their dinner would not spoil. Her belief was that if many people called, the problem would get resolved much more quickly than if only one person called. She also believed that most people don't bother calling because they think someone else will. Barry's day had been difficult, and he was uncooperative. Gillian again asked him to call, but he refused.

This upset Gillian, who felt she couldn't rely on Barry in a time of need. Making dinner by flashlight was very difficult. She wanted the lights to come back on as soon as possible, and so she took the time to make the call herself ... and their dinner was ruined.

Barry may have had a problematic day, but a blackout was no ordinary situation. He could have put his troublesome day aside and been cooperative. If he had helped his wife, they could have had a candlelight dinner and thoughts of his difficult day would have faded away.

Bob and Jennifer

Jennifer told me that when Bob retired, he began staying up late to watch TV in bed. She informed me that her natural body rhythm was to go to sleep by ten o'clock and wake up at six. She asked Bob to watch TV in the other room so that she could go to sleep by ten.

Bob was uncooperative and refused to get out of his comfortable bed and watch TV in the family room. Jennifer told me that she was forced to go against her natural body rhythm and stay up later than she felt comfortable with. As the months went by, she got into a new routine of going to bed late and waking up later. As a consequence, her whole daily routine changed, which caused meals to be later as well.

She explained that Bob preferred to eat all his meals early, so he started to complain. He had not anticipated the consequences of his own actions.

Being uncooperative doesn't just affect the immediate present; it may also affect the long-term future. And it will ultimately affect you, since a couple is essentially one—what affects one partner will affect the other.

My Space and Good Timing

We all need and have a right to space and time for ourselves—to relax, reflect, and restore. When your spouse wants time alone, you should not be offended; it's counterproductive not to respect his or her needs. During these times, instead of feeling left out, you can take the opportunity to do something for yourself.

Most men can focus on just one thing at a time. If his wife needs to talk to him and he is busy working on a project, she would be wise to practice her patience and wait for the right time. When he takes a break from his project, then he will be able to focus on what she needs from him. If she had interrupted him while he was working on his project, she probably would not have been successful and may have even created an argument. Timing is everything.

Here are some examples of good timing:

- after your spouse has eaten
- when he or she is not tired
- when he or she is relaxed
- when he or she is having a good day
- when he or she can focus on what you are trying to convey
- when you feel confident about what you need to say
- when you feel calm

Here are some examples of bad timing:

- before or during a meal
- when your partner is working on a project
- when he or she has just come home from work
- when he or she is in a bad mood
- when he or she is distracted
- first thing in the morning
- when you are hungry or tired
- when you are impatient or anxious
- just before bedtime

If there never seems to be a good time, then you can say to your spouse, "I really need to talk to you. When will you be available today?" or, "Can we talk in twenty minutes?"

During their menses, many women need time alone for themselves or to be with female friends. Her partner should not be offended; instead, he would be wise to take this time to work on his own projects or hobbies. Being patient and understanding of her need for space during this time is crucial. It is nature's way of physically separating a man and his wife so that when they reunite afterward, their passion will be renewed.

Health

Diet and exercise have a definite impact on relationships.

A bad diet can be the cause of a "foggy" mind, poor decision making, and irritability, which will be reflected in a negative attitude, causing challenges to become obstacles instead of opportunities. If you eat healthy foods, you will have a healthy body and a great attitude.

If you feel deprived by not eating certain foods, realize this: eating unhealthy foods deprives you of health, energy, vitality, a clear mind, and joy. These "foods" will ultimately cause you to feel depressed and to spend more time in a doctor's office.

A friend of mine knows exactly when her husband will be cranky and argumentative: after he has eaten fast food or sugary foods.

Skipping meals can create fatigue and irritability. Having one piece of fruit mid-morning and mid-afternoon instead of coffee and doughnuts can help you feel more balanced. Smaller portions and skipping seconds can help with weight issues.

When it comes to your body, it's more beneficial to be focused on being healthy, not on losing weight or looking a certain way. Eating healthy foods creates vitality, which enhances the peace and harmony in a marriage.

Couples can be a support system for each other by encouraging a good diet and becoming healthier together. Cooking healthy foods with your partner can be fun.

Inspire your spouse to start exercising with you. Walking around the block four or five times a week can be a start. Exercising together creates a bond between couples; they are doing something as a team. A lack of exercise may contribute to depression.

I've noticed, and I'm sure you have too, that after getting divorced, people often do a makeover on themselves: they lose weight, clean up their whole way of living, and make themselves look and feel attractive.

Looking and feeling healthy is appealing to others. To keep your spouse's interest, continue taking care of yourself so you will always be attractive to him or her.

If you want to improve your health and can't seem to do it on your own, visit *WellnessWithDrNikki.com* for excellent advice.

We Are One

A common mistake many couples make is not making space for each other in their lives. They continue to function from the place of "I/me." Once a couple is married, it's important that they evolve into a single unit, with the two "I's" becoming a single "we." They do not lose their individuality; rather, they expand to become a powerful partnership. In other words, they grow together as well as individually.

You need to include your spouse in your thoughts. If you usually think, *I like things done this way,* this thought needs to transform and become *I like things done in a way that's good for both of us.* You must do things that make your partner feel included; for example, when you turn down your side of the bed to go to sleep, you can turn down your spouse's side as well.

The following actions can help create the "we" in your relationship:

- If you are going to get yourself a snack, ask your spouse if he or she wants one too.
- When you grocery shop, consider what he or she enjoys eating and buy those items.
- Socialize together as much as possible at parties.
- Invite him or her to go with you when you go out.
- Consult with him or her before making any large purchases.
- Make decisions together regarding vacations and other important matters.
- Care about what's important to him or her.
- Be mindful of him or her.
- Take an interest in his or her activities.

*When a couple makes a commitment
with a Sacred Vow, the husband and wife
become each other's primary family.*

Friends and family are important, but your life mate must be more important to you. In most cases, your spouse's opinion must override those of family and friends.

It becomes clearer to a couple how much of a "we" and not two "I's" they are when something unfortunate happens to one of them.

Zoey and Jessie

Zoey told me that some time ago, she'd fallen and fractured her pelvis and was unable to walk for three weeks. Her husband, Jessie, had to take over the cooking, cleaning, and care of their two teenagers, as well as go to work every day, while Zoey healed.

Zoey said that Jessie complained every inch of the way. She usually had healthy snacks prepared for him, such as cut-up vegetables and fruit for whenever he felt hungry. She also usually packed him a lunch every day so that he didn't have to eat restaurant food. While she was healing, there were no healthy snacks or packed lunches. She said that Jessie was irritable and kept complaining to her. As uncomfortable as she was, she felt even more miserable with all Jessie's moaning. He was feeling the stress of not having his partner.

Zoey told me that after a few weeks, when she was able to get around and participate in family life again, Jessie told her that he had never realized how much she did to keep the family running so smoothly. The experience had made him very conscious of just how much of a "we" they were, and he was more grateful than ever for his partner in life.

Leave It in the Past

A mistake many couples make is keeping in the forefront of their minds memories of each other's negative behavior in previous years.

Your partner may not have been emotionally perfect for the first few years—who is?—but he or she may have grown, and past experiences may still be influencing how you feel about him or her now. There may still be a few kinks to iron out, but it's important to relate to your spouse as he or she is now and not based on history. This will reaffirm his or her new behavior.

If you continue to hold a vision of your life partner as he or she was, even though he or she may have grown, it will most likely cause discord in your marriage.

Romance

Romance can last a lifetime. To keep the romance alive, couples must keep their romantic focus on each other and avoid becoming too "familiar."

Avoid walking around in the nude. When you reserve it for intimacy with your spouse, nudity is far more exciting than if you have made it familiar—modesty is the best policy. Avoid watching TV in your underwear. Avoid leaving the door open when you're using the bathroom. Avoid belching or passing gas or being crude in front of your spouse.

Emulate the ways of courting couples. The idea is to keep improving yourselves and not let the relationship degrade once you are married.

Romance can be maintained by doing the following things:

- Flirt *only* with your partner and not with anyone else. This creates excitement in your relationship.
- Think romantically about him or her *only*, and not anyone else.

- Do romantic things, such as tucking a napkin with a heart drawn on it or a love poem in his or her lunch/pocket/briefcase.
- Open doors for her.
- Express how beautiful she looks when she's dressed up to go out.
- Always appreciate his chivalry.
- Compliment his or her style.
- Dress for him or her as well as for yourself.
- Go on romantic dates often.
- Be creative; for example, make your wedding anniversary and birthdays into special celebrations.

Romance is not just a matter of finding your spouse physically attractive. What is more important is the kind of thoughts you have about your life mate. Do you think, *My spouse doesn't turn me on anymore?* These kinds of thoughts are very destructive and must be eliminated.

Each couple should find a good balance of intimacy in their marriage—too little may not be satisfying, and too much may burn out a good thing. Think about this: if you indulge in your favorite treat every day, one day you may feel like a change. If you eat your favorite food only when you feel like having something special, you will look forward to tasting it even more.

Judy and Ben

Judy complained to me about Ben's "touchiness": he would touch her as many times as he could, 24/7/365. She said that when he arrived home, he would be touching her while talking about his day—she felt overwhelmed. I suggested to Judy that she try saying to Ben, "I love you and I enjoy your affection, but please think about this—when we show too much physical affection, it may eventually lose its specialness and excitement. Let's try to reserve touching each other that way just for when we are intimate."

Judy asked Ben some time later what he thought of her suggestion. To her surprise, he agreed with her, saying that he did experience more excitement by reserving the touching for when they were intimate.

When couples court, they make themselves look and feel desirable. It is even more important to make yourself feel attractive when you are married. In this way you will continue drawing your spouse to you.

Encourage anticipation when it comes to intimacy. When a romantic date has been set, talk with your spouse about your upcoming date—what you will wear (or not wear!), where you will go, and what you will enjoy about each other. It's more beneficial not to talk or think about work or the kids during romantic dates.

When it comes to intimacy, it is crucial not to fall into a routine, which can become monotonous.

Be creative and spice things up every now and then. Set the mood. Make private time: lock the door, switch off cell phones, close window coverings, and dim the lights. Burn aromatic candles, play romantic music, spray a favorite scent on the sheets. Whisper desires to each other, wear sexy lingerie, slow dance ... in the nude. Snuggle. Caress each other with a feather-light touch; be gentle and tender. Be in the here and now; make it intense, eyes and thoughts only on each other.

When intimacy in a committed marriage with the one you love and trust is carried out in a romantic manner, the aftereffect—that floating feeling—lasts for days.

Don't pressure your spouse into being intimate. If your partner feels pressured, intimacy will be a very negative experience, and he or she may push away.

Your partner is a human being, just like you are, and all humans have their good and bad days. Realize that your spouse may have different sexual needs than you do, and putting pressure on him or her will just make matters worse.

If your spouse never seems to be in the mood, rather than making him or her feel guilty or pressured, you can be gentle, tender, and enticing. You can be affectionate with hugs and kisses, or perhaps be patient and empathetic. Being loving and affectionate is very stimulating.

If your spouse does not even want to be touched, try having a gentle conversation to find out why he or she has pushed away. You can say, "We haven't been intimate for some time now. I miss being close to you. Is there a reason you don't want to be close right now?"

If your own libido has declined, you must not push away from your spouse to prevent intimacy. You must explain the problem to your partner by saying, "I know we haven't been close lately. Please don't think that it's you. I love you. My libido seems to be nonexistent right now for some reason. I would still love to hug you and be close in other ways, but please be understanding if we are not intimate right now."

Try massaging each other without the expectation of it ending up with sex. It's very important for couples to share with each other what feels enjoyable and what doesn't.

New parents sometimes forget that they are still husband and wife too. It's vital for a wife to keep her husband as the center of her attention even though she has children.

Sometimes when people become parents, their romantic passion declines. They place all their energy on raising their children. Kids do need attention, but ultimately they will grow up and leave home. Then it's back to being husband and wife. At this point, if the couple has not centered their attention on their marriage, they might feel like strangers or like they have grown apart.

Making romantic time for each other is extremely important to a marriage. Intimacy does not always have to include sex. It can simply be holding hands or sitting close while watching a movie. Romantic weekend getaways or even one-day outings without the kids are bonding experiences for a couple.

The Magnificent Hug

Believe it or not, a hug from our spouse—the person to whom we are devoting our lives, and vice versa—can be more intoxicating than any drug. It can be euphoric. Apparently, a hug from our life partner releases those "feel-good hormones," turning off stress and making us feel totally content.

A love-filled hug from your spouse
connects you to your soul.

Try this:

Hug your spouse and stay in each other's arms. Relax, close your eyes, put your cheeks together. Feel his or her warmth and breath. Slowly run your hands up and down your partner's back. Inhale each other's essence. Think about how much you love your spouse and how much he or she loves you. Stay that way for at least five minutes. When you separate, look into each other's eyes and see the love that you were thinking about and feeling from your spouse. You will automatically be smiling, because you will be experiencing that "love high," and you will feel even more bonded.

Hugging a life mate is an extremely important and very satisfying and pleasurable activity. If a couple is unaccustomed to being affectionate, they can start slowly and build up to a longer hug.

As with everything, the timing of a hug is crucial. Don't ask for a hug when your spouse is not ready, such as when he or she is distracted, preoccupied, or stressed out.

Be willing to make more time for hugging your life mate. The power of a genuine, soul-connecting hug is addictive. Try it—you'll love it!

What Are You Looking At?

"Looking" at other people is not without consequences. You might say, "I'm just looking! What's the harm?" However, doing so can eventually cause the passion between you and your spouse to decline.

Couples don't realize the disservice they are causing *themselves* when they look at other people. It is not just inconsiderate, rude, and disrespectful; it also damages their relationship. It may send an unintentional message to the other spouse: *I'm not satisfied with you. You are not enough for me. You are not good enough for me. I am still looking for my ideal mate, and when I see her or him, I will leave you.*

These are obviously not good messages for a life partner to receive. How could this person be happy in his or her marriage, especially if his or her parents divorced because of infidelity?

The habit of looking will cause a spouse to feel insecure in the relationship, and as a result, that spouse may not be able to love the "looker" in the way he or she desires to be loved. Receiving the message of being potentially abandoned may cause the spouse to close his or her heart (a form of self-protection) for fear of being devastated.

Looking may also have a rebound effect. If a woman feels emotionally insecure, she will not be happy. Guys, remember this very important rhyme: "Happy wife, happy life." Happily married men know this to be true. Since women are mostly responsible for setting the tone in the home, it will not be a happy one if the wife is unhappy.

If the husband feels emotionally uneasy in the marriage from his wife's looking, he may feel that he cannot satisfy her and look for comfort elsewhere.

In order for lookers to better understand the harm they are causing to their marriage, they should ask themselves these questions:

- Does my looking at other people make my spouse happy?
- Does my flirting with other people encourage my spouse to love me more?

- Does my behavior tear down my marriage or help build it up?
- Does my behavior build trust in my relationship with my spouse?
- If my spouse were the looker, how would I feel?

Our sages teach us that wherever our attention goes, our hearts will follow.

Looking can ultimately lead to fantasizing about other people. If this happens consistently and frequently, it can result in an empty marriage, adultery, and even divorce.

Standards and Expectations

When your standards are too high, your spouse may not be able to live up to them. You must also check to make sure that you are not creating standards that make it impossible for you to view your partner in a positive way. If your standards are too high, you will be setting yourself up for constant disappointment. You will also make your life mate feel like a failure, which may eventually cause him or her to give up trying to make you happy.

Make sure that your standards and expectations match up with reality.

Many people expect more from their spouses than they are capable of delivering.

John and Sharon

John complained to me that even though the economy was tough for everyone, Sharon expected him to maintain their current standard of living. John felt he was doing his best, but Sharon still wasn't happy. He said she was constantly trying to push him to find a better job with more financial security. John was just happy that he had a job! He was extremely stressed out, and he felt that Sharon did not appreciate the fact that in tough economic times he was still able to provide her with shelter, clothing, and food on the table. Even though they'd had to cut back on their spending in certain areas, they had the necessary basics.

Sharon's high standards had created tension between them. She needed a reality check.

Expectations that are too high work in a similar way. A spouse may eventually feel like he or she is not good enough and may give up trying. If you have expectations that your partner should make you happy all the time, you will experience disappointment. Expecting your partner to have automatic or intuitive knowledge of what makes you happy will put a strain on your marriage. Your expectations may seem obvious to you, but to your spouse, they may be puzzling. Letting your life partner know exactly what makes you happy simplifies the process.

Carol and Jeff

Carol explained to me that she was a sensitive person who needed kindness and gentleness. She said that coarse behavior was very hard on her nervous system and that her husband, Jeff, could be very harsh. I suggested to Carol that she make Jeff aware of this by saying (in her own words), "I thrive in our marriage when you are tender toward me; it makes me love you even more. Sometimes you can be harsh, and that causes me to be filled with anxiety so that I can't respond to you in an appropriate way." This approach would encourage Jeff to be more kind and gentle. I further suggested that when Jeff acted coarsely, she could say in a neutral but firm way, "That sounds harsh. I can't respond to you when you talk to me in that tone."

Informing Jeff of her sensitivity would help him learn how to make her happy, and it would also help him refine his negative tendency of being insensitive.

Daniel and Cheryl

Cheryl told me that she and Daniel had a morning routine that consisted of hugs and kisses and then breakfast together. She said that Daniel expected her to carry out their regular morning routine even when she was running late for an appointment—and he would become annoyed if she didn't. When Daniel was running late, however, he would hardly acknowledge that Cheryl was in the same room. This made her very unhappy. Daniel needed a reality check.

I suggested to Cheryl that she bring this out-of-balance expectation to Daniel's attention in a gentle manner by saying, "Daniel, I know you don't realize this, so I need to bring it to your attention. The other day when I was rushing to get ready for my appointment, I noticed that you expected me to participate in our morning routine and you became annoyed when I didn't. But when the tables are turned, you don't even acknowledge that I'm in the room. I understand completely—you are in a hurry! Please try to have the same understanding for me."

Daniel admitted that he had not been aware of his own behavior. Cheryl constructively helped Daniel refine a negative tendency of having unreasonable expectations.

It's best not to have the expectation that your spouse will change his or her bad habits just because you did. This expectation will create discord. You must not judge or criticize your spouse if he or she is not on the same path or growing at the same pace as you. Everyone is on a different life journey, and you must be patient and loving while your partner grows. However, some of your spouse's reactions may nevertheless change because he or she will be responding to *your* new behavior.

Difficult People

Some people say that the passion in their relationship has declined because they are married to a very difficult person or a person who is 90 percent great but 10 percent difficult.

There are some people who don't realize their behavior may cause marital difficulties. They have been functioning that way for so many years that it seems normal to them.

Natalie and Bill

Natalie told me that ever since she has known Bill, he has communicated in an extremely insensitive way during disagreements or when he wasn't getting his way. She said she was growing very weary of this treatment, which seemed to occur once or twice a month.

I asked Natalie to try to find out why Bill sometimes became "insensitive." She could do this by asking him questions about his life, as well as by taking notice of what happened before he adopted a difficult attitude. She discovered that his parents communicated in a coarse manner. Upon further investigation, Natalie observed that Bill's "difficult" episodes seemed to correlate with certain foods that he ate and when he was hungry.

I pointed out to Natalie that Bill may have learned his communication habits from his parents and therefore may not have been aware of them. To help him recognize the problem, she could say in a gentle manner, "You've mentioned to me that your parents were sometimes very coarse toward each other, especially when they were arguing. I think it's possible you may have learned from your parents, because sometimes you can be very insensitive when you communicate with me. I would like this to change; I feel it is very harmful to our relationship. We love each other, so let's work on being more pleasant, especially when we are disagreeing."

To help Bill overcome the problem of irritability that seemed to be related to food, we worked out a better eating plan. We eliminated from their diet all white-flour products, processed foods, fast foods, and sugar-laden foods. We added more fruits, vegetables, salads, healthy fats, and lean protein. I asked Natalie to have healthy snacks available for Bill when he felt hungry, such as cut-up fruit, nuts, celery and carrot sticks, raw cheese, and goat yogurt.

Bill and Natalie both felt much healthier and lost weight without even trying. Bill's difficult episodes seemed to magically disappear. Bill and Natalie transformed their marriage through their challenge.

It's not usually that easy to discover why a spouse can become difficult, so you need a shield to protect yourself at difficult moments. Getting into an argument when your spouse is not aware of his or her insensitive attitude just tears down the relationship.

Sometimes a simple one-line statement, said in a firm way without being emotional, will suffice. Here are a few examples:

- "I don't allow anyone to speak to me like that."
- "No! I will not allow you to treat me this way." (Then walk out of the room.)
- "Let's be constructive."
- "Let's talk later."
- "I don't want to fight with you."
- "I won't respond to an attitude like that."
- "I won't respond to such coarseness."

We all have our limits. You can't expect your spouse to always accept your negative behavior. You must not push your life mate to the edge. After all, you would not feel happy if your partner kept pushing you to your breaking point.

Sometimes, changing a pattern of communication
will transform the dynamics of a marriage.

Sheryl and Louis

Sheryl told me that her relationship with Louis was 90 percent great and 10 percent difficult. She said that sometimes he would speak to her as if he didn't even love her, which would make her feel hurt and defensive. An argument would then ensue.

I pointed out to Sheryl that when Louis became difficult, she could change the whole dynamic of that pattern by 1) not becoming defensive and 2) responding in a different way than she usually responded. She could say to him, "When you can talk to me in a good and kind manner, then I will respond to you," and then leave the room. She told me that she did exactly that, and a half hour later, Louis apologized.

Some spouses don't like change and will become "unconsciously" difficult to jeopardize it. They may even laugh, belittle, mock, become angry about, or ignore any attempts at change by their partners. Usually this is an indication that fear is involved—fear of change.

If your spouse does not like any variations from the familiar, even if it's for the good, you must be patient, kind, and gentle in implementing your new, positive changes. You must also be consistent and persistent: move forward, and he or she will respond. Your partner may not respond immediately or even in a month's time, until he or she feels safe and comfortable with the transformation.

A helpful book by Dr. Daniel Amen, *Change Your Brain, Change Your Life*, brings to light some "difficult" personality patterns.

Negative Cycles

An indication that a marriage is in a negative cycle is when the husband and wife feel irritated and impatient with each other's ways and quirks. When a couple is in a loving cycle, they are very patient with each other; those quirks seem adorable.

Negative cycles should not be allowed to continue, and couples must make an effort to bring their relationship back into balance as soon as possible. Very often, a spouse may resort to criticizing or complaining in an indirect effort to correct the direction of the marriage.

Criticizing and complaining are negative energies and will bring more discord, especially when they occur in front of other people. It is always best to be direct in expressing your needs; otherwise your spouse may misinterpret your desires or, worse, feel hurt by the criticism.

Both partners are accountable for their relationship being in a negative cycle. Therefore, each one must first ask him- or herself, *What is my part in the problem, and what can I do to get my marriage back on track?*

You may feel more loving sometimes than at other times, and that's when you need to be more vigilant in your thoughts, attitudes, and speech toward your spouse. It's almost impossible to feel loving when you feel negative, but you can still be kind.

Natalie and Sam

Natalie complained that Sam had been very distant and cold toward her for the past couple of months. She said that he seemed preoccupied and hardly noticed that she was around. When they did communicate, it was contentious. She felt their relationship was not in a good place, and she wanted to change things for the better. She said that this had happened before, and when she tried to correct it, Sam became argumentative and felt criticized and blamed.

I asked Natalie what her previous approach was, and she said she would say things like, "You have been on another planet lately. You are fighting with me about everything. When I talk to you, I have to repeat myself because you can't even hear what I'm saying. Do you even know that I exist?"

I suggested to Natalie that she try a more constructive approach by saying, "Things just don't feel right to me lately. Our relationship feels cold, and we fight about everything. Would you please help me figure out what's going on? I don't want us to be like this. I love you, and I want us to feel close again."

By saying that "*our* relationship feels cold" and not that Sam was cold, she lessened the possibility of Sam feeling criticized and shutting down. By using the word *we* and not *you* to discuss their fighting, she would establish that she and Sam were on the same side.

By using constructive means to bring Sam's attention to the fact that their relationship was in a negative cycle, she could help him refocus. He could then share his own concerns with Natalie

YOU CAN LIVE HAPPILY MARRIED FOR A LIFETIME

because he would feel safe from criticism. This would then bring a positive cycle back into their marriage.

When you need to bring something to your spouse's attention, you can say it in a constructive way that will not make him or her feel criticized, blamed, shamed, bullied, accused, or demonized.

For example, you could say, "Can I bring something to your attention? And this is not a criticism; it is just an observation...," or, "You are probably not aware of this, but sometimes...," or, "I'm just trying to help you by telling you this, all right? When you do...."

A destructive criticism would be something like this: "You are a horrible host. Why are you so antisocial? You are always on the phone, and you always leave me alone with the guests."

Here's a constructive alternative: "When we have guests, would you please refrain from talking on the phone unless it's urgent? I really don't like entertaining guests on my own."

If you don't feel loving, you can still communicate
in a kind and constructive manner.

You must also not be quick to be offended by what your spouse may say.

My husband and I were talking about women in leadership and how they are often labeled as "bossy." I mentioned that when I was growing up, people called me bossy too. My husband then said, "Well, you are stubborn." Huh! I had never been accused of *that* before. I felt a little stunned and irked at his statement, so I took a moment and thought, *Okay, so what is he trying to tell me? Maybe there is something for me to learn here.* I reminded myself that he is my partner in my growth, and I used my affirmations. Then I took a deep breath and asked him, "In what way am I stubborn?" He then said, "Well, *stubborn* is not really accurate ... *determined* would be a better word." I went instantly from feeling stunned and irked to feeling good. I liked that word. If I weren't determined, this book would not exist!

If I had chosen to become defensive, hurt, or confrontational, that situation would have turned out very different. Because I remained calm and questioned my husband's words in a neutral manner, we ended up smiling at each other instead of frowning.

The point is, we all have moments when we say something that may not be exactly true or may not come across the way we intended. If your spouse says something that bothers you, be patient and find out exactly what was meant instead of being quick to become offended or defensive, which can push your relationship into a negative cycle.

If you feel that your spouse said or did something offensive or inconsiderate, instead of becoming upset, you can say in a neutral way, "How would you feel if I said (or did) that to you?" Depending on how you say it, this will help your partner see your point of view.

Appreciation

Showing your spouse appreciation for the things he or she does for you and for your relationship will fortify your marriage. Someone who is shown no appreciation may feel taken for granted and, eventually, unloved. A person in this emotional state may unconsciously start to criticize or complain, become irritable or depressed, or find activities outside the marriage that he or she finds more stimulating and satisfying.

When you express appreciation to your life mate, you are essentially saying, "I see you—I see what you are doing for me and for us, and I am so grateful. I value you being in my life. I value you as my partner in life." Showing appreciation obviously builds a marriage. Your spouse will begin doing more of the things that you want him or her to do. Believe it or not, your partner really does want to please you. The more you express your appreciation, the more he or she may reciprocate.

It may sometimes be necessary to instruct your spouse about something you would like him or her to do. This is best done simultaneously with an expression of appreciation and always in the form of a request—never in a demanding way.

For example, you might say, "I really appreciate you helping me clean up after dinner. I'm so tired, and I find it very helpful. Will you please scrape the food off the plates before you load the dishwasher? Otherwise it gets all gummed up."

Notice that appreciation was expressed first, and then the request was made.

Routine

One of the things that will cause the passion in a relationship to decline is routine, which can cause a marriage to become mundane.

I know a couple that did the same thing every workday and the same thing on the weekends. They eventually divorced because, they said, their relationship had become routine and boring.

Change things, be creative, do something different and stimulating—have fun together!

Support

When you support your spouse in his or her interests, even if you don't find them appealing, he or she will feel your love.

It is beneficial to sincerely support and compliment your spouse when he or she is successful in his or her goals. For example, instead of saying, "Good for you—I'm happy for you," make it more personal by saying, "I knew you would get that promotion—you are so smart/skilled/talented, any firm would be happy to have you. Let's celebrate!"

The fact that your spouse reached his or her goal must be as important to you as it would be if it were your accomplishment.

It is equally important to support your spouse when he or she needs consoling. Instead of saying, "You'll get over it," try saying, "I know how strong and smart you are. I feel very confident that you will find a way to make things better."

Marrying Family?

Very often, people marry someone who subconsciously reminds them of or behaves like one of their family members. They will say, "I married my mother/father/brother/sister." These attributes were initially unnoticed, but they were always there.

Usually this happens because there are issues that the person needs to overcome, and his or her spouse will unknowingly present the person with the opportunity to do so. At the same time, the spouse can help the person refine related negative behavior. When such negative tendencies are dealt with, both spouses experience growth, which leads to a much stronger relationship.

Ester and Charlie

Ester told me that when she was growing up, her mother did not have a verbal filter and would call her "stupid" whenever she was upset. Ester explained that because of her experiences with her mother, she loathed that word and could not tolerate it when it was directed toward her. Ironically, Ester married Charlie, who used the word very freely and whose actions reminded her of her mother. Ester said that Charlie had never used that word toward her until one day when he was extremely upset and did not filter his words appropriately. Ester's "button" had been pushed, and she became furious and yelled at him.

I asked Ester if she had ever informed Charlie of the dynamics between her and her mother. She had not. I reminded her that Charlie was not a mind reader and that she needed to explain to him how her emotions were affected by the word *stupid*.

I suggested that she say, "When I was growing up, my mother called me stupid whenever she was upset, and it hurt me deeply. Please never use that word again when you are talking to me in any way whatsoever, even if you are angry. You will harm our relationship. It pushes my buttons and causes me to feel like I am about to explode. I love you, and I don't want to feel that way toward you."

By expressing her feelings in a respectful way, she set a boundary and made it very clear that she would not tolerate that word. Charlie understood that it was a sore point for Ester. He decided that using that word was not a very sophisticated way of expressing himself, and he eliminated it from his vocabulary. This helped Charlie refine himself.

Sometimes people who were abandoned by a parent will marry someone who becomes emotionally unavailable when upset, or otherwise "abandons" them in some way. They must learn that their spouse is not abandoning them, but rather, does not know how to deal with their issues of abandonment appropriately. The spouse who becomes emotionally unavailable must learn how to deal with challenges that arise and not emotionally (shut down) or physically (leave the house) "abandon" his or her spouse at those times.

He or she can also help mend old abandonment wounds by being more sensitive and saying sincere things like, "I will always be there for you," or, when leaving the house, "I'll be back soon" instead of "I'm leaving."

In some instances, you might think that you chose a spouse who is the complete opposite of your family members. But at some point, a familiar word, phrase, or action will surface. If you chose not to see the familiarity at the beginning of your relationship, it may irritate you until you do. It may take some time to identify it if you keep denying it to yourself.

When issues from your past are remedied through your spouse, you'll achieve tremendous emotional growth and your relationship will improve dramatically. When you refine yourself, your level of happiness increases immensely.

The more couples awaken and grow through the challenges in their relationship, the more their love will deepen.

I Trust You

One of the most important things that will build a strong marital foundation is trust. You must establish yourself as trustworthy, someone your spouse can depend on, and someone truly committed to your marriage for a lifetime.

Doing what you said you were going to do and being there when you said you were going to be there fortifies that trust. Trying your very best not to let your spouse down is crucial. You must help your partner trust that his or her emotional well-being is safe in your care.

For example, if you are angry, refrain from saying things that you know will push your spouse's buttons or that may be hurtful. You must not use your partner's past, or things that he or she has told you in confidence, against him or her.

When couples feel they can trust each
other, their passion thrives.

I Love You

Make sure that your spouse knows that you love him or her every day. By saying, "I love you," sincerely and often, you create good feelings in your marriage. You must also demonstrate that love by doing things your spouse will like and appreciate.

Have fun and laugh together. Taking part in pleasurable activities together, such as playing tennis or Ping-Pong, taking nature walks, going to the beach, and playing games, always brings a couple closer to each other. Cultivate your friendship; become best friends. Share different experiences—for example, when you come home from work, tell your spouse the joke someone told you at the office or that amazing story you heard.

Share happy stories instead of always discussing stressful situations. Focus on your life mate; look in each other's eyes while talking. Spotlight your commonalities.

You will find that when you focus more on the positive aspects of your spouse and your marriage, the negative aspects will not bother you.

Since you love and value your partner and you intend to remain together, you must practice patience. Patience refines a person. It is a noble yet humble quality to possess.

It is essential for couples to keep in the forefront of their minds what drew them together. They should ask each other what the initial attraction was. Sometimes if the marriage is in a negative cycle, recalling the beginning phase of the relationship can change it back into a positive cycle.

Reminisce about good times. Remember the good feelings you shared, and resolve to incorporate more of those into your marriage. Begin to do more of whatever activity created such positive feelings.

Paying attention to how you say hello and good-bye to your spouse is a very simple action you can take to make him or her feel loved. If it's possible (which it usually is—unless the children are in the bathtub, for example), you can literally drop what you are doing and walk over to greet your partner with a welcoming smile, hug, and kiss when he or she arrives home. Your spouse will feel that home is a place where he or she is loved, not just a place to hang up a coat.

When your spouse leaves the house, you can say good-bye in a way that shows that he or she will be missed. Remember that every time your spouse leaves, there is a chance that he or she may never return—unfortunately, accidents do happen. We have all heard the sad story of a grieving husband or wife who says, "I wish we hadn't been angry with each other! Now I can never say how sorry I am."

Looking up from whatever you are busy with—newspaper, project, cooking—when your spouse walks into the room shows that there is nothing in the world that is more important than your partner in life.

I Am So Grateful for You

Try this easy way to change your thoughts regarding your spouse:
Every day, write down one thing about your spouse for which you are grateful. By the end of the week, you will have several things on your list. Read it to your partner. Encourage him or her to do the same for you. Make it a ritual that you both do four or five times a year. If your spouse doesn't like the idea, don't pressure him or her to participate; you can still do it for yourself.

We often take the positive things our spouse does for granted and then hold on to the negative things that were said and done. Whenever you find yourself ruminating about your spouse's contrary words or actions, read your gratitude list instead and focus on his or her positive attributes.

You Are Worth the Effort

If a couple doesn't make endeavors to rekindle their passion, it will eventually die. But by making an attempt—and sometimes it doesn't take much—they can ensure that their passion will begin to burn brightly again. When each spouse is a "rock" for each other, the moon could fall down and they would still feel safe and whole.

The more effort you put into your relationship, the hotter your passion will burn. When it becomes a roaring fire again, you will say to yourself, *I can't believe I let my marriage go like that! I would have lost so much. I am so grateful that I woke up in time!*

Key Points

- Know that rekindling your passion is not as difficult as you may think.
- Habits, ways, and patterns that are detrimental to your marriage must be changed—beginning with you.
- Learn how to balance periods of growth with having fun together.
- One of the most important assets to your relationship is keeping a positive mental view of your spouse.
- Having a negative view of your partner distorts every aspect of your marriage.
- Comparing your spouse to any other person is not recommended.
- Respect is imperative for a good relationship.
- Accept your life mate's ways that are different from or even contrary to your own.
- Be willing to cooperate with your partner.
- Diet affects your health and marriage.
- Make sure your standards and expectations are realistic.
- Make your spouse's dreams and interests important to you.
- Overcome childhood issues through your partner.
- Prove yourself trustworthy to your spouse.
- Become best friends with your spouse.
- Have an attitude of gratitude toward your life mate.
- Every ounce of effort you put into your marriage raises the level of passion.

Chapter 7

Everlasting

There she sits on the couch, her knitting needles clicking rhythmically. He's comfortable in his big, cushy armchair, reading his newspaper. The years are starting to show—a silver strand here and there and smile lines deepening. He feels her looking at him, turns his head and catches her gaze. There's no need for words; the look on her face tells him that her love for him is true and pure. His heart swells with his love for her, and his emotions rise up to his face, causing him to smile. He places his still, strong hand over his heart, reciprocating. Her eyes close with contentment for a moment as she continues knitting the sweater she is lovingly making for him. The newspaper rustles as he turns the page, that special smile never leaving his face.

♥

There comes a time when we become more settled in that journey called life. Then, just when we think we have it all figured out, life sends us a curveball. We all should be aware of the changes that take place later in life. If we aren't, they will take us by surprise and our marriage may pay the price.

Most people are familiar with the term *midlife crisis*. But the fact is, midlife changes only become a crisis if we are uninformed.

At this point in life, a marriage can be either the most cherished thing in a person's life or something that the person would like to end. It all depends on whether the couple has been nurturing and building their relationship or tearing it down.

This is also time to do the "weeding"! All the issues that each spouse has found irritating will surface around this time and must be weeded out, no matter how small or insignificant they may seem. Discuss them in an amicable way, with the intention of resolving them, accepting them, or trying to understand them from your spouse's point of view. Be willing and cooperative—this is your life.

Couples who have been building their relationship for the most part will now know what it's like to have a true partner in life, someone who cares deeply about them, who wants only the best for them, who considers their life, happiness, and well-being as important as their own. They are best friends; their love has grown and strengthened over the years. They have discovered the true meaning of love.

Despite their flaws, they love, respect, and accept each other. They trust and rely on each other. They can't imagine life without each other; they have each other's back. They realize the value of their life partner. They have learned to resolve challenges without damaging their relationship, because their marriage is the most important thing in the world to them.

If the passion in your marriage has declined, making that extra effort at this stage in life is essential. You can't see the good in your marriage when your thoughts of your spouse are negative. Destructive thoughts and actions create many obstacles and resentments. These patterns must be discontinued and replaced with new, more positive patterns.

*A key to successful marriage is for the couple
to realize that the bond that was created
with their Sacred Vow is everlasting.*

Let's take a look at some of the issues that may arise around this time of life, issues that could possibly derail a long-term relationship.

Hormones

A change in hormones can dramatically affect a person's marriage. Being informed about our bodies and how they change is a very important step to maintaining lasting peace in the home.

Staying away from certain foods before menses, such as caffeine, junk food, sugar, and spices will help diminish PMS. Intense discussions should also be delayed until the woman's hormones are more in balance.

When women are young, their hormones allow them to tolerate issues that could otherwise cause irritation or annoyance. But with the onset of perimenopause, a woman might find that she can no longer tolerate these issues and feels overwhelmed by the slightest stress. Understanding these feelings will help her realize that it may not be her husband or her career that is making her angry, frustrated, sad, or depressed.

I know a woman who called a family meeting with her husband and two kids to discuss her changing hormones. First she educated herself, and then she shared her knowledge with her family. From then on when she seemed "hormonal," her family knew exactly what was going on and what to do for her and themselves. She had complete support from her family, which enabled her to be harmonious in her transition.

When a woman feels hormonal or is experiencing a hot flash, intense discussions should be postponed until she regains her composure. She must not be embarrassed or afraid to say to her husband, "Let's discuss this later—I'm feeling a little overwhelmed right now."

Some men don't want anything to do with "women's stuff"; they just can't relate, and they don't feel comfortable discussing it. At these times, friends and support groups will help ease the transition.

Dr. Lynne Walker has a number of great books to help women become educated about their bodies, including *Menopause and Estrogen, Breezing Through the Changes*, and *A Woman's Complete Guide to Natural Health*.

Men go through hormonal changes as well. It's a myth that midlife changes are strictly a "woman's thing"—after all, men have hormones too. Men's hormones decline at a much slower rate than women's, and so the changes may not seem as apparent. However, at some point in their lives, men may experience anger, irritability, restlessness, aches and pains, fatigue, depression, muscle loss, hair loss, low libido, anxiety, and other symptoms of reduced hormone levels.

Besides the emotional fluctuation that midlife changes may produce (these could start as early as age thirty-five), a person's thinking may start to change as well. Men and women may become hypercritical or cynical and blame their spouse for their mental and physical discomfort. Their partner's flaws may appear magnified, and it may become more difficult to focus on his or her good qualities. When this happens, it becomes easier to lose sight of the many, many years that were spent building a marriage. A long-term relationship may unravel if the couple is not prepared for the changes that everyone experiences in middle age.

It is therefore up to each of us to monitor our thoughts. It's crucial at this time to keep your focus on the positive and not to allow negative thoughts to overtake you. Destructive thinking can ruin a marriage.

I know of so many couples who have destroyed their lives because they thought it was their marriage or job that caused them to feel the way they did.

When hormone decline (in men or women) creates anger and anxiety, it's helpful to drink calming teas such as passionflower, chamomile, and valerian. You can clean up your diet by eliminating all unhealthy and processed foods. You can start exercising, which helps alleviate stress. It would also be beneficial to learn how to manage stress and practice some type of meditation.

If couples focus their attention on their marriage as they age, the husband can become the patriarch of his family—a trusted and wise benevolent leader. The wife can become the cherished star, with her intuition and feminine guidance.

When we learn that hormonal changes are a part of life, we can then accept the physical and mental changes that come with it. Aging is inevitable for everyone. It's the normal process of life that commands that we come down from the top of the mountain so that the next generation can have their turn.

Today, many people view themselves as not being useful to society once they reach their senior years. This is an incorrect perception, because in fact the opposite is true: history has demonstrated that families and societies are much more successful when they value wisdom and guidance from their elders.

Being an elder is an honor that is truly earned. By the time people reach this point, they have seen more, done more, experienced more than anyone from the younger generations. It's their time in life to start sharing the wisdom that they have attained through their life experiences, in order to help others. In reality, they've become even more important than they were.

During difficult times in the aging process, you and your spouse must support and remind each other, "It's just normal hormonal changes—we are doing just fine." Smile, even if doing so feels incongruent with how you feel on the inside. If you keep at it, one day you will realize that you are smiling on the inside as well.

If you need help, read *You Are Not Alone* by Prudence Hall, MD, founder and director of the Hall Center in Santa Monica, California, and a pioneer and expert in the field of regenerative medicine and hormone balancing.

Pushed Apart

As people age, sometimes the libido and its respective organs no longer function as they once did; at some point everyone will experience this change. That does not mean that the couple is losing interest in each other, or that they've reached the end of physical contact. Sometimes just being touched, lying in each other's arms, hugging, or just holding hands with your life mate can be extremely comforting and satisfying. It's important to your marriage that you make the effort to continue with some kind of physical contact.

With hormonal decline, however, some people no longer want any kind of physical contact. Their concern may be that it may stimulate their spouse's desire to be intimate. They may then be barraged by destructive thoughts regarding intimacy and their spouse, essentially turning themselves and their spouse off. This pushes the couple apart and may be the cause of significant marital challenges.

Even though one person's libido may have diminished, his or her spouse's libido may still be vibrant. Let's take, for example, a woman and a man, both aged fifty-five. Many woman experience low libido and menopause at this age, while a man's libido may still be vital. A man's biology allows him to procreate into old age, although his libido may start tapering off at age forty-five.

The spouse with the low libido can approach his or her partner and say, "My libido isn't what it used to be, but we can still hold each other. I'm very willing to please you in other ways, but we may not be able to be intimate every time. I love you, and I still want to be close to you."

At this point, it's crucial not to develop what I call "anti-spouse" thinking—that is, criticizing (in your own mind) how much older your partner may appear—because most likely you have signs of aging as well. This is another unconscious way of pushing your spouse away.

It's important for both partners in a couple to realize that their spouse is the person they chose to spend their time on this earth with. They must therefore be willing to remain physically close in some way. (See "The Magnificent Hug," chapter 6.)

Being physically close to your life mate is soul-satisfying.

If you and your spouse have pushed apart because you are no longer intimate, becoming physically close again after having been separated for some time may feel uncomfortable at first. Start slowly. Do something fun together: play a contact game, hold hands, embrace, nap together, be in each other's arms for at least a few minutes each day. Try to make a physical connection every day in a way that feels comfortable for both of you.

Longstanding Challenges

If problems in a relationship have been allowed to continue for a long period of time, one or both spouses may at some point feel suddenly overwhelmed, like they can no longer continue in the marriage.

Debbie and Sol

Debbie and Sol had been married for twenty-seven years, and they had three grown children. Debbie told me that when Sol became frustrated, he verbally abused her (a negative tendency). She said that in the past, she would justify his actions by making excuses for him—stress at work, etc. She felt that she was reaching a breaking point. She explained that the last time Sol took his frustrations out on her, she suddenly "exploded" and screamed at him to leave.

Sol said that he was completely taken by surprise because Debbie had never mentioned anything about how she felt. He said he loved Debbie and was not willing to end their twenty-seven-year relationship without fighting for it.

I explained to Debbie that she had *enabled* Sol's behavior toward her rather than helping him learn how she would like to be treated (a negative tendency). She needed to express herself in a calm way and not let her emotions build up to the point of "explosion." I suggested that she express herself in an informative way: "Sol, I understand that you become frustrated sometimes. You are probably not aware that you are also abusive at those times. This hurts me very much. I'm your wife; I feel very disrespected when you behave like that. It also damages our relationship. I am asking you to become conscious of your behavior and maybe reframe your thinking or take a walk—just don't take it out on me, because I will not allow that anymore. I need to know that you understand what I'm saying."

Sol admitted that he was not aware of his own negative behavior. He understood that Debbie had reached her limit and that he had to become conscious of his pattern and change it. Debbie realized that she could have ruined their marriage with her outburst. Through this challenge, they both transformed negative tendencies in their personalities.

If your partner behaves in a way that causes you discomfort, irritation, or offense, you must bring this to his or her attention. Negative emotions that are allowed to accumulate will eventually cause resentment. Ultimately, *your* behavior toward your spouse will be contrary, creating a negative cycle in the relationship, or an "explosion."

It's very important to realize that your partner may not be aware of his or her negative behavior. For this reason, it's vital to bring your spouse's attention to this conduct in a constructive way and teach him or her how you would like to be treated.

If your spouse seems to become upset easily or tends to overreact toward you or certain situations, you can help your partner realign his or her thoughts by saying things like this:

- "It's okay—it's not so serious."
- "What's really bothering you about this? You seem to be overreacting."
- "This is small stuff. Why are you getting so upset?"
- "Relax—it's not the end of the world."
- "You are overreacting. Stop for a moment and take a breath."
- "You need to reframe your thinking".

Keep trying different words until you find the ones that work. *How* you express those words makes a difference.

Allow yourself to be influenced by your life partner; he or she is trying to help you. You can also learn from your spouse's ways. For example, if your partner stays calm under stress, ask how he or she does it: what mental pep talk does he or she use to remain centered?

My friend's husband is an "overreactor." To help him realign his thoughts, my suggestion to her was to use *his* words ("It's okay—it's not a big deal.") so he would immediately calm down. When she used his language, he instantly connected to what she was saying.

Empty Nest

Children grow up and leave home to begin lives of their own—this is healthy and inevitable. Some children may even move to a different state or country. If a couple has made their children the center of their attention, they will experience a feeling of emptiness and loneliness when their children eventually leave home.

The most effective way to prevent these empty-nest feelings is for the husband and wife to remember that even though they are parents, they are first and foremost life mates. They will then be able to provide a powerful center within the family from which healthy children can be raised. This will also provide good role modeling for the family's future generations.

If the couple has accomplished this, then when their children finally leave home, the couple will not be strangers to each other.

On a positive note, when the nest is empty, the couple will have more time to have fun together and do things that they have been wanting to do. If necessary, they will have the opportunity to start courting again and rekindling their passion.

Drainers

If some problems are allowed to continue unresolved, they will eventually drain the relationship. Some examples are workaholics, friendships with the opposite sex outside the marriage, needy friends, emotional abuse, chronic complaining and criticism, constant disapproval, drug or alcohol abuse, inappropriate attention to other people, and comparing a spouse to others.

When couples collaborate to remedy a challenge in their relationship, they can overcome it, and as a result they will refine themselves, build a stronger marriage, and be more powerful together.

Aches and Pains

At this stage in life, aches and pains can be an issue, which can cause irritability. At these times, it's important to realize that your spouse is not responsible for your discomfort; therefore, you must do your best not to take your frustrations out on him or her. Remembering that your partner may also have aches and pains will also inspire you to have more compassion.

It's always best to control your reactions toward your life mate when he or she is feeling irritable. You can never know the reason until you investigate. You can inquire with concern, "How are you feeling today?" You may find out that your spouse did not sleep very well the night before, or is feeling bad, or has some ache or pain. When you exhibit empathy, it shows that you care, and hopefully your partner will then use restraint with his or her frustrations. You can also inquire if there is anything you can do to help. Compassion and a hug can sometimes be the cure.

The Golden Years

I read a beautiful story on the Internet that brings home this point.

An elderly man goes every day to visit and have lunch with his wife in a nursing home. She has Alzheimer's and can't remember who he is. One day, the nurse asks him, "Why do you make the long trip every day? She doesn't even know who you are anymore." He responds, "Yes, but I know who she is."

Can you just imagine the deep caring and love this husband and wife had, and still have, for each other? This is a couple that definitely made their marriage the center of their attention. They learned from their challenges and created a bond so strong that nothing, including a devastating illness, could separate them.

As we age and possibly start to lose our mental and physical health, our lifelong partner will watch over us.

Many years ago, I was extremely grateful to have the opportunity to witness two different lifestyles of two elderly couples in the same day, just moments apart. To me this was not a coincidence, but rather a divinely inspired happening allowing me to witness two different outcomes.

Let me explain. Whenever I see an elderly couple, I always like to start a conversation during which I ask them how many years they have been together. If it looks like they have a good relationship, I'll ask what their secret is, and they always seem to relish talking about their time together.

I was at the farmers' market when I noticed an elderly couple bickering over a head of lettuce. He was talking harshly to his wife about getting one head instead of two. The look on his face was one of total disdain and contempt. Her face had a tired, pained look, and she was complaining. The way they communicated was very unpleasant. I found out that they had been married for sixty years.

How awful! I thought. *This is not what I would call the golden years.* I walked away from them feeling very sad.

Moments later, I observed another elderly couple sweetly talking about the oranges they were inspecting. They were looking into each other's eyes and smiling. He made a joke and she laughed. They walked off arm in arm, still smiling and laughing. The way they communicated was very loving and gentle. This couple had been married for fifty-two years. Their secret was being best friends, showing mutual respect, and sharing 100 percent accountability for the success of their marriage. These were definitely the golden years for this couple—they were going out with glad hearts. My role models!

What an incredible difference there was between these two couples. I could see that physically, both couples most likely had aches and pains, except the second couple were not taking it out on each other. Instead, they were lovingly supporting and taking care of each other. They understood that they were partners in this journey, so why not make it a good one!

The first couple could still have changed their ways; it's never too late. The man or woman could have said, "I don't want us to live this way anymore. I want us to live in peace and harmony. I want us to go out with smiles on our faces. We had a good relationship once—we can do it again." They had probably accumulated many bad habits over the years and obviously needed to change their patterns of communication. Then they would have to be persistent and consistent in their new ways. Every time things became negative, she or he could say, "This feels destructive. Let's be happy people."

When it comes to our emotional well-being, we tend to be overprotective and resistant to change.

Your spouse may object to or resist some of your new, positive ideas. If you are kind, consistent, and persistent, your partner will eventually see that the changes are good and will ultimately like the new way of functioning and communicating.

Be a Role Model

You can be a role model for your life mate. By showing kindness and gentleness so that your partner can experience them, you may encourage your spouse to change his or her ways.

If your partner is the type of person who doesn't easily notice things, then you can bring it to his or her attention—"Have you noticed how kind and gentle I am toward you?"—and then say, "I'm being a role model for you! Does it feel good to you?" Most likely, the response will be yes. Then you could say, "It would make me very happy to experience that also. Let's be kind and gentle toward each other from now on—agreed?" Reminders will sometimes be necessary.

I'll Watch Over You

There is an elderly couple in our community center, and at one point the wife became extremely ill. She needed surgery, medication, and assistance with all her daily activities. Her husband dressed her and did her makeup and hair so that he could bring her to the community center each week to be with friends and people she knew. I observed how attentive he was; he constantly had his eye on her. One day I said to him, "Your wife is so lucky to have you." His reply completely overwhelmed my heart: "No, I'm lucky to have her."

This woman was very ill for many years and could not possibly have given anything in return to her husband, yet he was the one who felt lucky! With her husband's tender loving care, this woman is now recovering her strength and is slowly getting her life back. Without him, I believe, she may not have made it.

This is what it's all about: building a love, a bond so strong that when you can't be there for yourself, your life mate will be there with you, lovingly taking care of you, watching over you. What an incredible feeling that is! As we get older, our spouse becomes even more important to us and to our survival.

Having a committed partner in life—someone who has been through thick and thin with us, especially as we age—fills our life with meaning and purpose, which creates health and longevity.

Keep On Trying

A key to successful marriage is to never stop trying to improve the relationship.

The way to improve your relationship *is* there—if you seek it, you will find it. If you stop trying, your marriage will almost certainly decline. Worse yet, you will miss your opportunity to refine yourself so that you can reach your full personal potential.

Marriage is a partnership. Each partner must hold him- or herself 100 percent accountable for the state of the relationship. Every ounce of effort made toward creating harmony in the marriage will make an impact.

Think about this:

Let's say you and a partner open up a new business together. You are both excited, and you both work really hard to set up the business, investing an enormous amount of time, energy, and money. Each of you has a different set of skills and talents that will make the business successful. Finally you have your new offices and all the equipment you need, and you are all set up to start doing business. Would you both then put your feet up on your desks and say, "Okay, now the business can run itself"? How long would your new business last? Not very long!

We invest an enormous amount of emotion, time, and energy in our potential life mate. We have glorious weddings and honeymoons, and then shortly thereafter we tend to let the relationship "run itself" as children, work, stress, and other life events distract us.

If you've made the important decision to change your relationship for the better, don't expect it to improve overnight, or even in a week or a month. It is possible that it could change almost instantly, but if you have spent many years tearing it down, it's crucial to be patient and never stop trying different ways to build it up again. A marriage is not like a computer, where you can press a button and reboot it. If you are persistent and consistent, however, change *will* happen, and your love will be better and stronger than ever.

Unfortunately, some couples judge each other in an increasingly negative way the more years they spend together. They build a mental case against their partner (anti-spouse thinking), and in time their thoughts become over-exaggerated, distorting reality. They then focus primarily on each other's flaws, which eventually causes an unconscious distancing.

Consider asking yourself, *Why am I thinking these thoughts? What lack within me is causing me to judge my spouse so harshly?*

All great teachings admonish us not to judge another person simply because we ourselves are not perfect. Most of us overlook and justify our own shortcomings and mistakes but judge our spouses rather harshly for theirs.

The more you focus on the *positive qualities* of your life partner, the fewer challenges there will be in your marriage. And if you are active in building your relationship, even less discord will occur. A marriage requires nurturing and attention to be healthy and successful.

If you think that you have tried everything to help your marriage but nothing seems to be working, realize that you just haven't found the right solution yet. Become more open to seeing your spouse's point of view; try communicating in your partner's language; try doing the complete opposite of what you have been doing while always remaining kind and compassionate. Brainstorm together: try something completely new, be creative, focus on your marriage. It's worth it!

Make the decision to keep trying different things until you find what works. If you make the attempt, you *will* find the way that will lead to harmony. Don't think that it will never happen. The very next thing you try could be the magic formula, and the potential of your dream will then be realized.

Key Points

- Remember that the bond that was created with the Sacred Vow is everlasting.
- Changing hormone levels can negatively impact a marriage if the couple is uninformed about and unprepared for them.
- Maintaining physical closeness is very important.
- Longstanding issues, if allowed to continue, will eventually cause resentments to accumulate.
- To prevent empty nest syndrome, make your marriage the center of your attention.
- Be aware of issues that can drain your marriage of vital energy.
- Be a role model for your spouse.
- Never quit trying to improve your relationship. The very next thing you try may be the magic formula.

Chapter 8

In the End

There they stand once again, under a canopy of soft, white, fragrant flowers—he's still dashingly handsome, and she's still glowing. It's now their diamond anniversary. As she looks into his softened eyes, a rugged smile appears upon his well-worn face. Her silver locks are tied up in a neat little bun on the top of her head, one strand flowing down the side of her cheek. Their faces reflect the wisdom of their years together; they've cherished every moment. They have made the most of their marriage. They have grown, and their love and friendship for each other has deepened to become a vast reservoir from which they can draw. The beautiful light that surrounded them on the day they took their Sacred Vow seems more golden than ever, imbuing with awe their extended family and friends who are looking on. They turn and face their guests, who jump to their feet—smiling, clapping, and inspired with hope.

♥

Ultimately, the destiny of your marriage lies in *your* hands. Every couple has the ability to create the kind of marriage that they initially dreamed of.

> *A key to successful marriage is making the commitment to stay married for a lifetime.*

When you have this intention, you realize that marriage is a "forever commitment." This inspires you to put forth your very best efforts, and it benefits *you* greatly. The more you put into your relationship, the more *you'll* get out of it and the happier *you* will become.

It's imperative to transform your initial romantic emotions into an everlasting love. You can do this by nurturing your love for your life mate and eschewing any contrary thoughts.

The Consequences of Divorce

Divorce has a tremendous impact on the fabric of society. Strong, stable and peaceful societies depend on the well-being of the family unit.

What we do as individuals affects everyone and everything around us for generations to come. While the full impact of today's unprecedented divorce rate is yet to be recognized, we do know that many of today's young people have a very different view of marriage than their grandparents did. Many children today were born out of wedlock and are being raised without the family unit role model.

The divorce rate for second marriages is higher than that for first marriages. People may have higher expectations going into a second marriage, putting a strain on the new relationship. Stepchildren and ex-spouses complicate matters. Many people have expressed to me that they regret not having tried harder in their first marriage.

Humans were created to be in lifelong, monogamous relationships.

History shows that people are healthier and live longer when they are in a committed marriage. They are also psychologically and emotionally stronger.

Bonding with one's spouse is fundamental to a successful marriage.

You Have the Power

If you feel your marriage is not working, know with certainty that you can turn it around and immediately start building it up. You have the power to stop tearing down your relationship and start improving it.

The potential for your marriage was there in the beginning and is still there now, waiting for you to get back on the path that will lead to it.

You can do this using the suggestions in this book even if your spouse is uncooperative and not on the same page of life as you. When your life mate sees your endeavors to improve your marriage, he or she will respond.

There's no better experience in life than the feeling of being loved and giving love! Be willing to try and keep on trying.

A key to successful marriage is realizing that your spouse is in your life because he or she wants to be with you.

Your spouse wants the same things you want. Your partner wants to be loved by *you*, to feel important to *you*. Your life mate wants to matter in *your* life. It's also important to your life partner that you are happy and that he or she is contributing to your happiness.

Remember that your spouse is the one *you chose* to help you reach your full personal potential. You intuitively knew that your partner was *the perfect one* for this incredible task. You can reboot your memory by recalling what drew the two of you together in the beginning. As soon as you recollect these initial emotions, your marriage will start changing for the better.

Successful and happy couples are totally committed to each other. Their intention is to be together for the rest of their lives. They don't compare their spouse to anyone. They know that they are better in this world together than they were on their own. They hold themselves accountable for the condition of their marriage; therefore, they are always working to improve themselves and their relationship. They never let their marriage get off track for too long. They don't allow friends or family to influence how they think or feel about their life mate. Their partnership allows them to feel secure and peaceful.

Distractions

As humans, we are naturally influenced by materialism. That said,we must not allow ourselves to be distracted from reaching our potential.

Your spouse is your soul mate as well as your physical partner, and your marriage is the most important relationship you will ever have. Remembering this, will eliminate most of the temptations from any distractions.

Let In the Light

Darkness cannot exist where there is light.

A key to successful marriage is seeking
peace and harmony in your relationship.
Then the negatives will fade away.

Make a conscious effort to create peace and harmony in your marriage. They will spread to every part of your life and can go on to transform the world.

All esoteric teachings encourage us to be kind, gentle, cooperative, and harmonious toward each other. It's crucial not to judge your spouse harshly or expect perfection from him or her—no human is perfect. Each day with your life partner must teach you how to live in a more loving manner.

If you keep tearing down your relationship, it cannot last for a lifetime. If you consistently work on building it up, it will thrive. Be willing to do whatever it takes to get your marriage working again, even if it means getting out of your comfort zone. This will greatly benefit *you*.

If you want your marriage to reach its potential, you can't wait for it to happen; *you* must initiate the transformation. And now, with this book, you can!

You can choose to live with love and harmony
in your life and in your marriage.

A small act of kindness can transform someone's life.

᠅

The author believes that we can transform the
world by being kind and helping each other.

᠅

A portion of the proceeds of your purchase of
this book will go toward helping others.